Almost Hired

ALMOST HIRED

WHAT'S *REALLY* STANDING BETWEEN YOU AND THE JOB YOU WANT

JACKIE DUCCI

LIONCREST
PUBLISHING

ALMOST HIRED

What's Really Standing between You and the Job You Want

ISBN   978-1-5445-1399-7 *Paperback*

978-1-5445-1400-0 *Ebook*

To those along my path who recognized that still waters run deep. This one's for you.

CONTENTS

INTRODUCTION

You worked hard in college and earned a great education. You've been in the workforce for a couple of years, or even decades, and gained valuable experience. Perhaps you even got promoted recently. You know you are a skilled professional with a lot to offer. You've polished your resume and have been applying for new positions over the past several months in hopes of landing an exciting new opportunity. But despite all your efforts, not one employer has presented you with an offer. Not. One.

Perhaps you've gotten a few phone calls or interviews, but that was where it ended. Each time, you received a polite email informing you that another candidate was chosen—with no explanation as to why. You just can't seem to convert all your hard work into an actual offer. All those late nights spent applying to openings and preparing for interviews, and nothing to show for it. Each time, you're left wondering what you did wrong, what you could be doing better—and worst of all, why someone else was "better" than you.

You're feeling frustrated and questioning your worth. You're thinking, "I'm smart, capable, and motivated—why doesn't anybody want me?! Why am I not good enough?"

You are not alone.

A recent study by Glassdoor.com found that for any given opening, 98 percent of applicants never hear back from the hiring agency. That means only 2 percent do. That's a pretty staggering statistic.

Is the job market really so chock full of exceptional candidates that only the cream of the crop stands a fighting chance? Are your credentials subpar? Are you hopelessly undesirable to employers, for reasons you'll never even know because no one will just level with you? Or are you making the classic mistakes of a typical ill-informed job seeker?

I don't know you, but I can almost guarantee it's the latter.

Have you ever noticed that the elusive, magical top 2 percent seem to find themselves in that position over and over again? We all have that one friend or acquaintance who always seems to be in demand, whether they are actively looking for a new position or not. When they put themselves out there, they effortlessly land interviews and offers. The kicker? Even when they are satisfied at work and not looking for a new position, headhunters are calling *them* right and left. What makes them so special? Why are they so sought after?

You might be tempted to think these people are just incredibly talented with unmatched experience, work ethic, and skills. Maybe. Maybe not. I would bet that the number-one skill they have mastered is the *job search process* itself.

Here's the problem. This whole job-seeking thing—you're doing it wrong. There is nothing lacking in you as a person or as a candidate. The problem lies in *how* you're going about finding your next position.

BEWARE OF BAD ADVICE

Sadly, candidates shoot themselves in the foot every day, at every stage of the process. They follow advice from their career counselor, or their friend, or some nugget of generic "conventional wisdom," without realizing that the advice (nine times out of ten) is actually terrible. By applying it, they are inadvertently blowing their chances of getting hired.

There are many career coaches and counselors out there who dispense cookie cutter, counter-productive advice that haunts people for decades. Their guidance may be genuine and well-intended, but it's often not applicable in the real world. In fact, it may even hinder a search rather than help it. It is very common for students to graduate college armed with practice interview questions, a resume template, and the results of some cliché "what career is best for me" test, and absolutely no idea how to actually find a job.

A LEARNED SKILL

There are a few dozen classic mistakes, most of which the general public knows nothing about—and many of which I can practically guarantee you are making. The good news? They can all be easily avoided once you know what they are.

What I have learned throughout my career in the hiring

world is that *job seeking is a learned skill.* And it's a skill that anyone can master—including you.

What does that mean, exactly? It means you don't have to be the best, the smartest, the most talented, or the most qualified applicant in order to get the interview and the offer. You just need to master the process.

In fact, that's the reason I am writing this book: to help good people like you land the positions that they deserve. If you follow my advice, you will start securing employment offers before you know it—by job seeking the right way.

QUICK FACT

You don't have to be the most qualified applicant to be selected for a position. You *do* need to understand what hiring managers really want, so you can use that knowledge to outsmart the system.

WHY LISTEN TO ME?

I am a headhunter. I get people hired for a living.

Throughout my professional career, I have placed hundreds of candidates successfully in new positions, and coached thousands in their job searches. I support companies daily in their hiring processes and have collected fifteen years' worth of firsthand data on how employers make *actual* hiring decisions. What criteria they look at, what they consider to be red flags, what they like and don't like, and all the other insider information they never reveal to candidates—I know it all. I hear it all. I live it every single day.

My clients are the companies doing the hiring, so when they choose to hire or reject a candidate, they tell me exactly why they made that decision. I'm privy to the truth about why candidates are being turned down—and it sure isn't sugarcoated. This priceless information is the missing link for job seekers all over the world. It's the secret information that everybody wants, but nobody gets access to. A company can be honest with me as a third party in the hiring equation, but they are almost never honest with candidates.

> **DEFINITIONS**
>
> *Client:* When I use the term "client," it refers to a company that is hiring.
>
> *Candidate:* When I use the term "candidate," it refers to a job seeker.

It is easy for candidates to feel frustrated when they are rejected and the company won't tell them why. If applicants knew why they didn't get offers, they could use the detailed feedback to improve for the next time around. I am here to divulge this inside information, completely unfiltered, from the trenches of an employment agency.

How and why certain candidates get passed over while others get hired is actually completely predictable. When I screen candidates for an open position with one of my clients, I know within the first thirty seconds of speaking with someone whether or not they are going to get hired. Yes, I'm serious. There is tremendous consistency in what companies consider to be an "ideal" candidate, so much so that I instantly recognize it when I see it. Believe me when I tell you that the criteria used to evaluate people is not what you think.

> There is tremendous consistency in what companies consider to be an "ideal" candidate, so much so that I instantly recognize it when I see it. Believe me when I tell you that the criteria used to evaluate people is not what you think.

NOT JUST ANY JOB

But just landing any old job offer isn't really your goal, is it? It might be a fun ego boost, but not your end game. Your real goal here is to find and secure a *great* job. You deserve a position that suits you, at a company you feel happy and proud to work for, and where you can see yourself staying for many years to come. It turns out that, just like job seeking, finding the *right* job is also a learned skill that anyone can master.

When a candidate executes their search process thoughtfully and skillfully, applying real-world advice, they reap the rewards that come with better employment—a higher salary, career advancement, increased happiness, a better corporate culture, more work-life balance—whatever their objectives may be. Helping people land successfully in new positions and changing their lives for the better as a result is one of the most fulfilling aspects of my career.

WHO SHOULD READ THIS BOOK

If you are struggling for traction in your job search, this book is for you. I wrote it for candidates who are feeling stuck, confused, and overlooked—to the point where the issue has become systemic.

Perhaps you are a recent college graduate who can't convert the advice you received from career services into a concrete job offer. Maybe you never obtained a college degree, and you're worried that's the reason employers aren't taking you seriously. Maybe you are mid-career and looking to move up in title, or to change career tracks completely, but making it happen has been more difficult than you expected. Perhaps you love your job but want to find a better corporate culture. Maybe you're a mom who took a few years off to have a family, but you are now finding that your time spent outside the business world has been a hurdle to overcome when applying for positions.

Your age, experience level, title, industry, personal situation—none of that matters. The rules are the same, and yes, you've come to the right place. With a little bit of coaching and a new perspective, you too can become a job search superstar. Apply the strategies in this book, and before you know it, *you* will be in the 2 percent, attracting interviews and offers. You'll be the one your friends look at and think, "She scored such a great job—how did she do it?"

A FUNDAMENTAL SHIFT

It is also important to note that turning yourself into an ideal candidate does not necessarily require going back to school to obtain an advanced degree (or any degree at all). This book will address fundamental shifts in your technique and strategy that anyone can apply immediately.

Most candidates approach their search from the perspective of, "Let me tell you all about *me* and why I'm so great." That makes sense, right? In order for a hiring manager to like you, they'll need to know everything you've done and how amazing you are.

In the real world, however, that's actually not an effective strategy. To win at the hiring game, you need to flip the script. Successful job seekers are masters at considering the hiring process *from the point of view of the hiring manager.* In other words, don't make your approach about *you*, make it about *them*. That shift in mentality is a major component of what distinguishes competitive candidates. It is a surefire way to stand out, even over those more qualified than you. But what does it mean exactly to make the hiring process less about *you* and more about *them*, and how do you do it?

This book will walk you through the entire process from A to Z, providing insider tips and proven strategies that actually work. We'll begin in Chapter 1 by addressing one of the most overlooked components in all of job seeking: how to identify the *right* jobs. This alone will increase your success rate exponentially. In Chapter 2, we'll look at what you should do before you apply. Chapter 3 will give you an insider's look at what happens to your application once it's been submitted. Chapters 4 and 5 explain how to navigate your interviews and some of the final-stage curveballs that you might encounter. Chapter 6 delves into how to evaluate an offer. And finally, Chapter 7 explores working with a third-party hiring agency.

By the time you've read all seven chapters, you will have the inside scoop on what really goes on in the world of hiring every single day. You'll clearly understand what you've been doing wrong and how to course-correct those mistakes of the past. This book will enable you to attack your search with fresh energy, newfound enthusiasm and genuine confidence. Most importantly, you will see results.

I suggest reading the entire book from start to finish, although each chapter is designed to stand on its own and can be read in any order. For example, if you typically have no problem getting interviews, but you never seem to get a second one, you might want to skip to Chapter 4. If you recently got an offer and you're wondering what to do next, read Chapter 6. You may not want or need to read the book cover to cover. But if you do, you'll see how all the information is tied together into one cohesive system.

When you show up to work every day feeling energized, fulfilled, and happy to be there, life is grand. You can feel it, your family will feel it, your friends will feel it—heck, even your dog will feel it (I'm a dog person). I promise you, learning and applying the skills and strategies in this book will be worth every minute you invest in it. The payoff is huge.

Everything is about to change. Are you ready to get started?

Chapter One

STOP APPLYING FOR THE WRONG JOBS

The instinct of many active job seekers is to apply to an exorbitant number of job postings. They think, "I'm going to put my resume in front of as many employers as possible until something sticks." It's tempting to do this, particularly when you are anxious to get out of your current situation, or you're unemployed and desperate for a paycheck. But this shotgun approach is not an effective strategy.

Any job search can spiral into a disorganized, haphazard scramble if the candidate doesn't have clear objectives from the start. In this chapter, we'll talk about why it's much better—and more productive—to execute a focused, intentional search that only targets openings likely to be a good match for the applicant *and* the employer.

A little introspection, self-assessment, and analysis on the front end of a search will pay off in spades, saving you from getting down the wrong path. Too many job seekers hit the ground sprinting in a bad direction, only to find themselves very unhappily employed (and clueless as to how they got there) a few months later. Obviously, you want to avoid this, but you probably don't know how. This chapter will show you.

IS THERE REALLY SUCH THING AS A *WRONG* JOB?

Yes! It is very possible to get hired into a new position and regret it instantly or very soon thereafter. Sadly, it happens to people all the time. Choosing the wrong job results in a depressing sense of unmet expectations, frustration, and regret.

It's easy to see how this can happen. Getting caught up in the flattery of an employer showing interest in hiring you is natural. Let's face it, it feels good to be wanted. Your phone rings, and the caller wants you to interview for a position. You're not initially feeling excited about it, but you say yes anyway. You've been sending resumes and putting yourself out there with no concrete return for months, so you feel compelled to see what this opportunity is all about. You go to the interview. Before you know it, the company has fallen in love with you, and you find yourself at the end of the process being presented with an offer—maybe your *only* offer. You should be thrilled. But you're not. Something doesn't feel right.

Despite your gut screaming at you, "Don't do it!" you convince yourself it's a good move. Anything is better than staying in your current situation any longer, right? You accept the position. You reason with yourself, "It's the only offer I have after all this time, so I'd be foolish to say no." Or, "If I turn this down, how do I know if or when another one will come along?"

A few months down the road, you're miserable. You know you made a big mistake. You have a new position, but you're just as unhappy now as you were before. You wonder, "How did this happen?" Now you're actually in a worse position. As soon as you start interviewing again, the first question potential employers will ask is why you only stayed at your current company for six months. You'll be fighting an uphill battle that could have been avoided.

A WORD ABOUT CAREER TRAJECTORY

Before we get into the nitty-gritty of how to ensure you are applying to the right jobs, I want to touch for a moment on the issue of career trajectory. I know this is a tough pill to swallow, and one that many people would prefer to turn a blind eye toward, but here is the truth: the earlier in life you commit to a specific career track, the better off you will be.

I often hear the exact *opposite* advice given to college students and entry-level professionals. It makes me crazy. The "guidance" typically goes something like this: "You have time! Try a bunch of different careers until you figure out what you like. Take a crack at sales. Do administrative work for a year or two. Explore hospitality. Build houses. Travel the world. It'll make you look well rounded. Eventually you'll figure out which career is for you."

No, no—a million times, no.

Employers hate this. Nothing turns a hiring manager off faster than a resume that shows zero trajectory in a specific industry or discipline. A list of unrelated careers across different industries—even if each one has value in its own right—is a no-go zone. The best-case scenario that employers want to see is a logical career trajectory, ideally within one field.

Now, of course most people are going to have a couple or a few career hops, especially in their twenties. It is true that there is value in different experiences, and very few people know exactly what they want to do coming out of the gate. It's not impossible to get hired if your resume lacks a focused career track.

If your path has been more meandering, don't panic. We've all been confused and experienced a hop or two, or three, early in our careers (myself included). The point is, the sooner you can figure it all out and commit to a specific path, the better. Here's why: those candidates who demonstrate logical trajectory are consistently favored over those who do not. It's just an important reality to be aware of.

> Candidates who demonstrate logical trajectory are consistently favored over those who do not.

If you must change jobs or industries while you're in your exploratory phase, *be intentional about it*. Don't just jump for no reason; be thoughtful about the changes you are making, and why. Act with a purpose—not haphazardly. The more well thought out your actions and explanations are, the more unlikely a hiring manager will be to see them as red flags. In the next chapter, we'll talk in depth about how to most effectively package your experience.

A superb resume in the legal world might show a bachelor's degree in political science, to a first job as a paralegal, to law school graduate, to first-year associate at a law firm—all focusing on a specific type of law (let's say mergers and acquisitions). For any law firm looking for a mergers and acquisitions attorney, that resume will be favored. The candidate will absolutely be contacted to set up an interview—and probably fast-tracked through the hiring process.

An unattractive resume might show a degree in accounting, an entry-level role in pharmaceutical sales, a second position doing administrative work, and an objective explaining that the candidate is currently in pursuit of their real estate license. That's a major head-scratcher for any hiring manager, even if the position they're hiring for is accounting, or pharma sales, or administrative, or real estate. With no clear idea about which track the candidate is committed to (if any), or which one she is best suited for, the resume just looks like a messy hodgepodge of random experiences. Trust me, the hiring manager will pass.

Another harsh truth is that changing careers is difficult. The farther down one track you are, the harder it is to get employers to take you seriously when you express your desire to switch. Just ask anyone who spent ten years in human resources and decided they wanted to change to graphic design. Theoretically, it could happen, but that person will have a tough road ahead obtaining the skills necessary and convincing any graphic design company to bring them on board. Even if they did land somewhere, they'd likely have to start at the bottom of the graphic design world. That's a steep price to pay for someone in their thirties.

It's also important to note that people choose all sorts of career trajectories for all sorts of reasons. For some, it's important to genuinely love what they do. They want to identify a vocation that will bring them a deep sense of fulfillment. Others care less about the "feel good stuff" and are driven by money; they choose a path based on how they can accumulate as much wealth as quickly as possible. Others feel drawn toward particular trades, such as carpentry or cosmetology. Some go into a family business because there is a path there already laid out for them.

When it comes to choosing a direction, there are thousands of options, with all sorts of motivating factors—and no wrong answers. The key is to select something that works for you (and that you can stick with) as early in your career as possible, whatever it may be. If you do, you'll stand out among the pack. Employers will perceive you as grounded, reliable, and self-aware—all great qualities that any company would value in its employees.

WHAT DO YOU WANT TO BE WHEN YOU GROW UP?

The pressure of selecting a career track can be overwhelming, intimidating, and confusing. Luckily, there are excellent resources out there that can help you figure out your best direction. This is not one of those books.

But I do encourage you to seek assistance in your quest. The best thing you can do is utilize a combination of tools (books, online assessments, etc.) and look for overlapping results. Note the themes, personality traits, and so on that resurface for you consistently as you review your analyses.

Also, take assessments and "what should I be doing with my life?!" books with a grain of salt. Treat each result as a navigation waypoint, and one insight among (hopefully) several that will be meaningful to you. Your big "A-ha!" is unlikely to come from one single source. The more you consult and explore, the more you'll learn and dig up clues to the answers you are seeking.

Once you identify a recurring theme, take note—that piece is a critical component of your ideal career and trajectory. Maybe it has come up on multiple assessments that you are an independent person who does best taking ownership of your own projects. The takeaway is that you need autonomy at work. Avoid positions that will force you onto team-oriented tasks or where you might be micromanaged.

TAKE TIME TO DECONSTRUCT

So, how do you begin figuring out your next best move? To avoid ending up in an unsuitable position, you must get to the root of what has caused you to be happy or unhappy in your current role, and in your past jobs. Spending time on some deep career and self-analysis is important *before* you begin a new search. Let me explain my suggested method.

Start by reflecting on your previous work history. If you are fresh out of school and have not held full-time positions yet, consider your internships, summer jobs, part-time work—any professional experience you have to date. The exercise will be just as effective.

Take out a piece of paper or open a new document on your computer and list every position you have ever held. Under each one, list bullet points describing what you liked and disliked about each position. Really think back to how you felt when you were in those roles, and at those companies. Did you wake up every day looking forward to going to work? If so, what aspects made you feel that way? Or did you dread Mondays? If so, why? It is important to think three dimensionally, so be sure to consider each position from every possible angle. Consider responsibilities, advancement opportunity, corporate culture, length of commute, work-life balance, size of company, compensation and benefits, relationships with coworkers, company mission and values, and so on. Literally anything you can think of that added to, or detracted from, your happiness and job satisfaction. When you're finished, go back over those lists and study them.

What worked for you? What didn't? You might find that your own answers surprise you. Maybe the jobs you loved all have some of the same characteristics. Maybe the positions you hated, you hated for similar reasons. People sometimes think they are unhappy in a job for one reason, but after analyzing the situation, they realize that the root of their problem is actually something deeper or different altogether. Getting clear about what works and doesn't work for you is essential—*before* you begin your search. That's the only way you'll ensure you don't put yourself in an environment just as unsatisfying as the one you're trying to leave.

> Getting clear about what works and doesn't work for you is essential—*before* you begin your search. That's the only way you'll ensure you don't put yourself in an environment just as unsatisfying as the one you're trying to leave.

Once you get a handle on your needs, let that knowledge guide you in selecting which openings you pursue. For example, if you hated one position because your commute was miserable, don't apply to anything that isn't close to home. Or maybe you didn't get along with your boss. What were the characteristics about that person which caused the two of you to clash? When you're interviewing, you'll know what kind of personality traits to avoid in a future boss.

Always consider the responsibilities you've had in previous positions. People do best in roles where they can focus on tasks they enjoy. If you hated spending endless hours manipulating spreadsheets, make a note of it and avoid any job that requires you to live your life in Microsoft Excel.

Also keep in mind that positions with similar titles can have vastly different responsibilities. For example, it's common for roles like an executive assistant to be totally unique from one company to the next. Maybe you're an executive assistant (EA), and you love handling the professional tasks (drafting correspondence, booking travel, keeping calendars, interacting with clients, etc.), but you feel uncomfortable with personal requests, such as dropping the children off at school or picking out personal gifts. (You wouldn't believe the stories some EAs have about the tasks they've had on their plate. Finding a Tinder date for the boss? True story!) Some people don't mind handling personal items, but others do. Everyone is different. Get clear about your own preferences and boundaries.

The goal is to assess opportunities through a new lens, empowering you to only go after the ones likely to be a good match, while avoiding any position that has a high potential to lead to dissatisfaction.

Company size and the number of employees on a team or in a department is another important consideration that is often overlooked. Large companies tend to have more structure, bureaucracy, and management layers, which is great for some personality types but frustrating to others. Likewise, some people love the informal atmosphere and camaraderie of a small, team-oriented startup, whereas others can't function optimally in that setting. Which environment would you prefer?

You should also consider company culture and the personalities of your coworkers. Some corporate cultures work hard and play hard together, and their relationships extend into each other's lives outside of work. Some cultures are very formal and conservative, whereas others are relaxed and laid-back. Do you like private offices? Or do you prefer open, collaborative work spaces? There are so many factors to consider. Think about the environment you would feel most comfortable in, based on the ones you have enjoyed or disliked based on past experience. Choose a company with a culture that feels like a genuine, natural fit for you.

What about core values, living your life's purpose, and "finding your why?" Do you want to work for a company that has a bigger, altruistic mission—like fighting poverty or bettering the environment? Or maybe that greater sense of purpose is irrelevant for you, and you're more interested in the paycheck, perks, and advancement opportunities that an organization can provide. Either mindset is perfectly respectable. The key is to know what's important to you, embrace it, and select potential employers accordingly.

If done right, this self-analysis takes time. But trust me, it is time well spent. After you make your lists, study them. Note patterns and consistencies. Identify deal-breakers. Make relevant notes and put a star next to the most prominent points. Really take the time to sit with this exercise and ruminate on it. I know some of you are thinking, "Okay, whatever, I can skip this." Don't! Completing this process is a crucial step on the path to finding your ideal position. Take your time here. Really process your findings. What you uncover will be meaningful.

DETERMINE YOUR NON-NEGOTIABLES

The final step is to distill your lists and notes into what I call your non-negotiables list. These are the insights and the takeaways that are the most powerful, and that you will not budge on. Non-negotiables can include things you absolutely must have and things you simply will not accept.

For example, some people may decide that having weekends and holidays off is non-negotiable. Maybe they have a family, and their "off" time on Saturday and Sunday is dedicated to activities with their children. Or perhaps the person is actively engaged in a sport and attends associated games or competitions every Sunday. Working weekends is not an option in these scenarios. By contrast, someone else who does not have weekend commitments may not care about working on weekends and might even prefer to have their time off during the week while the rest of the world is at work.

Every position you apply for should pass through this filter of your non-negotiables. Write them down, keep them in a prominent place where you will see them every day, and commit to yourself that you will adhere to them.

The whole point of this exercise in deconstruction is to provide you with a compass for navigating future career choices. If you've spent enough time in thoughtful self-analysis, you'll have a real leg up in identifying ideal career opportunities. Equipped with your new guide, you'll be ready to identify and select opportunities that are best suited for you.

WHERE HEAD MEETS HEART

People tend to approach a job search one of two ways—logically or emotionally. A purely logical decision maker might look only at the numbers and the facts—title, salary, bonus, hours, number of vacation days, the black and white bulleted job description, and so on—without much consideration of how the role would make them *feel*. An emotional decision maker might focus exclusively on whether or not they get a warm and fuzzy feeling at the prospect of working there, without much regard for whether or not the logistics make sense. Both approaches have their place, but neither by itself is enough.

CANDIDATE CASE STUDY: JESSICA

Jessica is a candidate whom I worked with a couple of years back. She was a very smart entry-level professional, but she never did any self-assessment. She applied for a sales role with one of my clients, and I was excited to submit her for the position because she checked every box that the company was looking for. I instantly loved her energy during the screening process. She was so likeable and articulate, and she also managed to convince me that sales was the career for her. I couldn't wait to introduce her to my client. Sure enough, they hired her.

While Jessica was a fit for the position itself, the role and the company weren't a fit for her. At her core, Jessica was an introvert. She could crank up her energy and make sales calls for a couple of hours or so, and while she was great at it, the function was tiring to her. It went against her natural way of being.

After a long day on the phones, interacting with people constantly and forcing herself to function outside of her natural skillset, Jessica was exhausted and unhappy. She couldn't wait to just go home and curl up on the couch. Unfortunately, that didn't mesh well with the company's culture. Her sales manager and her team were all extroverts, who went out together after work and attended all kinds of social gatherings and industry events. "We'll see you at happy hour," was a phrase constantly heard around the office. Meanwhile, it made Jessica want to roll her eyes or hide under a rock every single time. When she turned down the majority of these invitations, she was pegged as anti-social and not a team player. She was ostracized as a result. It was really unfortunate that her coworkers didn't take the time to get to know the real Jessica, but the culture simply was what it was—and she was an outlier.

Needless to say, the job and the environment wore her down to the point where Jessica just couldn't do it anymore. After a few months, she burned out and quit in pursuit of other sales opportunities more geared toward long-term relationship building rather than dialing for dollars, and in environments with a more mature, less collegiate culture. Eventually, she did land a new opportunity that was a much better fit. But it took a while. Having to explain a position that only lasted several months to future potential employers was a major hurdle in every single interview. Not ideal.

Jessica's story is a classic example of what happens when someone accepts a position that they're not well suited for. Jessica knew she was an introvert, but she never did a deep dive into her own likes, dislikes, and comfort level. Her need for solitude and a more "chill" group of coworkers were aspects that went unexamined before she applied for the position. She had never considered how the introverted side of her would be stressed and strained in that sales role, as good as she was at it from a proficiency standpoint. If she understood herself better, she would have avoided that position and wound up in one that was a better fit altogether, from the get-go.

I encourage you to factor both head and heart without allowing either to overpower the other. The jobs that make logical sense for you *and* make you feel excited are the magical opportunities that you should be pursuing full steam ahead. Make them your focus, always, and you'll be in excellent shape.

> The jobs that make logical sense for you *and* make you feel excited are the magical opportunities that you should be pursuing full steam ahead.

KNOW WHAT YOU'RE GOOD AT

There is an important final overlay to this entire exercise: your skills. You must know what you are good at (and what you're not). Are you a fantastic writer? Do you struggle with numbers? Is relationship-building where you shine? Do you panic when you have to give a presentation?

Each of us has our strengths and weaknesses. If you pursue a role that does not align with your natural talents, the outcome will be unsuccessful. No matter how much you may love to sing, if you're tone deaf, you're not going to make it as an opera or Broadway performer! If you try to be something you're not, you'll just wind up feeling miserable, underutilized, and not good enough. Focus on positions that will highlight your strengths.

BE PICKY

By being selective about the opportunities you apply for, your odds will improve. You'll also save a lot of time.

You've just invested a ton of time learning more about yourself and building your short list of non-negotiables. Now, you must put the information to good use. Refer to your notes constantly. Stick to the guidelines that you have set for yourself.

For each individual job, ask yourself truthfully, "Does this position sound like a good fit based on my skills and experience *and* based on my needs? What about based on the company's needs? Is this a match?" If the answer is yes, you should apply. If it's no, or even a "not really," move on.

If you hate your current job, it's easy—and understandable—to feel anxious to get out and find a new one. Hard as it may be, resist the temptation to pursue anything that is just plain not a good fit. The odds of you getting hired are effectively zero, and even if you do, it won't be a position that you'll want for the long term anyway.

IF YOU'RE UNEMPLOYED, STILL BE PICKY

If you're unemployed, it's easy to feel desperate and take a job (any old job) so that you have the security of an income. I get it, the rent is due.

But here's the problem: if you jump at the first opportunity that comes your way, you're likely to make a choice that you won't be happy with long term, and then you'll find yourself in a cycle of job-hopping that will hurt your career in the long run. I know it's hard. But if you're unemployed, it's still in your best interest to stick to your non-negotiables list and be selective. Stressed as you may be, force yourself to think further down the road and play the long game.

WHERE TO LOOK FOR OPPORTUNITIES

The savviest candidates diversify their search to land the best possible job. If you attack your own process from multiple angles, you will yield a much higher rate of return than you would if only relying on a single tactic or resource.

ONLINE JOB BOARDS

These days, the first instinct of most job seekers is to look for jobs online. Yes, the application numbers are staggering and the odds are stacked against you, but you are missing out on opportunities if you do not utilize job boards as a component of your job-seeking efforts. Online applications should have a place in everyone's search—particularly if you follow the advice in Chapter 2, which will position you to be in the 2 percent of applicants who get noticed.

As you skim online postings, remember that job descriptions are generally not arbitrary or made up. They are the result of time and effort on the part of a hiring manager. If something is included in the job description, there's a reason for it. So it's important not to disregard the content of the posting.

Candidates sometimes say, "Well, maybe they didn't mean what they wrote in that description. Maybe that's not really a requirement." If it's in there, it probably is meaningful to the company and important to the role. Remember, the person writing the description is getting paid to find qualified candidates that will succeed in the position. They're not trying to mislead applicants or attract anyone who won't be a match. Out of respect for their time (as well as yours), respect the job descriptions and assume that they were written thoughtfully, and for good reason.

What if you have everything a position requires except a couple of items they "prefer?" Do you apply? I say yes.

Frankly, this phase of the search is about common sense. If you're missing eight out of ten of the mandatory requirements, you're wasting your time. But if you have all of the mandatory requirements, or even the majority of them, then it makes sense to go for it.

Look at the whole picture, and always remember that *some* of the items in job descriptions are probably negotiable. If a posting says five years of experience minimum and you have three or four, I'd say it's still worth applying, because sometimes those numbers are thrown out as a guide, not a hard requirement.

Nevertheless, it's critical that you be honest with yourself. If a posting sounds like an amazing opportunity that you would love, but you know deep down that you are nowhere near qualified, you know what to do.

Pay attention to the language used. Read the job description with enough respect for the hiring manager not to completely deviate from the stated requirements but also realizing that there is probably some flexibility. For example, some postings say, "A college degree is required." But they may just want to attract college graduates, without the degree being an actual requirement. There's no way to know for sure how rigid certain components are, but if you have enough years of experience to make up for the absence of a college degree (or other aspects you are lacking) you might just get an interview.

> Read the job description with enough respect for the hiring manager not to completely deviate from the stated requirements but also realizing that there is probably some flexibility.

Maybe the company wants a degree in journalism, but yours is in English. That's pretty damn close, and I would encourage you to apply. Step back and look at the big picture. Pay attention to word choice. Are they saying what they absolutely require or what they strongly prefer? Is a qualification listed as a requirement but doesn't seem to be essential to the role when you read the bulleted job description? That might indicate negotiable space. Be honest, be reasonable, and follow your gut. Here's the key: Don't chase pipe dreams, but don't pass up good opportunities either. Know and recognize the difference between the two.

YOUR NETWORK IS EVERYTHING

Your network can be your best source for quality job leads. Human connections have the potential to get you on the fast track for positions that you may otherwise never have had a shot at, and it prevents you from being just a random resume among a sea of others. A nod from another living, breathing person will automatically elevate you out of the pack and into a small group of personal recommendations. Eyes will be on you faster, and your resume will be evaluated with greater diligence. Networking goes a long way toward improving your odds. And to some extent, job seeking is a numbers game.

Any candidate referred by someone on the inside is far more likely to be granted an interview—whether they're as qualified as the other applicants or not. Sometimes this is because the hiring manager feels an obligation to the person who made the referral, or because there is a level of trust there. "If so-and-so recommends this person, even though their resume isn't perfect, maybe there is more to him than meets the eye." *That*, my friends, is the power of a referral.

I have clients who tell me, "Don't post our openings online. We only want to see candidates you already know personally." My clients could easily post their own job openings and instantly create their own pipeline of potential employees to pick from. But they want candidates that come recommended from a trusted referral source (me), who I already know and can vouch for from personal experience. Why? Because hiring a personal referral is less of a gamble for the employer; rather than a stranger, they are hiring a friend of a friend.

Young professionals in particular are often reticent to turn to their connections. I have never understood this. What is the hesitation? Your network is the greatest resource that you have. Use it! Oftentimes in life, *who* you know is more powerful than what you know. Take advantage of your own relationships and use them to get ahead. That's not nepotism, that's just networking.

How do you start? Go through all of your contacts. Look through your phone, your email, your LinkedIn and other social media. Make a list of anyone influential in any way who may be able to give you a leg up, an introduction, or even advice about how to get your foot in the door. From professional contacts to mentors, internship connections, to friends—the people who know and care about you want to help you. They want to see you do well. There is no shame in reaching out to them. Heck, they'll probably be happy to hear from you. So hit up your network (again, smartly, and selectively), and don't be shy about it.

One caveat to remember when networking: If you are currently employed, it pays to be discreet. You don't want your employer to find out that you're looking to leave. In sensitive situations where confidentiality is of the utmost importance, be selective about who you approach for help. Only network with people you trust or who have a high likelihood of being able to help you. Put the message out that you're open to new opportunities, but do so thoughtfully.

WHAT IF I DON'T HAVE A NETWORK?

Everyone has a network. Even if you think you don't, you absolutely do. Once you start making that list of contacts we just talked about, you'll be surprised at how many people you know.

Even if you are young, I guarantee some of your college classmates are working for desirable companies. Contact them. Get creative. Look up former teammates from sports or intramurals. What are they doing now? Where are they working?

Networks extend beyond friends and family. Have you done an internship? Think about who you encountered during that internship. And don't forget people from school. Teachers, coworkers, vendors—those are great prospects for networking.

For the non-entry-level crowd, the same advice applies. Turn to your friends, your friends' spouses, contacts you have from charity boards or organizations you belong to, former colleagues and bosses, your kids' friends' parents, you name it. You never know where a great lead will come from, so do not rule anyone out. Think outside the box.

Identifying your network is one of the smartest things you can do. Most people don't, which is really unfortunate, because networks make all the difference. If you take advantage of yours, it will set you on the fast track to your next great opportunity.

CAREER FAIRS AND CONFERENCES

I know, you are probably rolling your eyes right now at the prospect of attending career fairs, conferences, industry events, and the like. The truth is, they can be a gold mine for identifying new opportunities and meeting potential employers. Take them seriously.

Think of it this way: When you're applying online, you're sending a resume, the goal of which is to get you some face time. If you have the opportunity to meet people at a live event, you've just bypassed stage one completely. That gives you a huge advantage.

For example, if you want to work in human resources, big HR conferences are a great place to meet people, put yourself out there, and begin to build a network. After a panel discussion, go up and introduce yourself to the presenters. Build a rapport. Ask for their business card, tell them that you are actively looking for a new position, and keep in touch with them after the event. They just might think of you if and when their firm is hiring (or they know of another one that is).

Here's another truth: people help (and hire) people they like. If you make a positive first impression, that hiring manager is likely to invite you to interview, or tell some-one else, "This person is worth an interview." Boom! Instantly, you've just bypassed the hardest part of the hiring process—getting noticed and on the radar.

When you make the effort to go to a conference and meet someone in person, they see you as a real person, not just a meaningless piece of paper. Envision yourself networking in your desired industry. Attend conferences and meet people. Go to career fairs with your resume in hand. Be polite but persistent.

DO YOUR RESEARCH

Always learn as much about a potential employer as you can, and begin gathering information before you apply. Doing this diligence early can save you lots of time and energy—and prevent you from inadvertently getting down a rabbit hole.

Start on the organization's website. It won't show you everything about them, but it will give you a good starting point. Look at the way the company represents itself online. Read the bios of the key employees. Does it feel like you could fit in with them? What's the vibe? Check out the company's mission statement. Does it resonate with you? Does the culture seem like a good fit?

For more senior roles, like manager or director, you will eventually want to know all of the specifics about the group or team that you will be leading, the current and future projects at hand, and so on. But at this early stage, everything you see online will help form a gut feeling about this potential employer.

You can dig deeper, if you are feeling especially motivated. If you know someone who works, or formerly worked for, the company, make a phone call. Find out, "What is it really like? Are you happy?" Ask questions. Someone who knows the company from the inside will be your best resource for true insight.

Also take a hard look at any factors that relate to your non-negotiables. Can't deal with a long commute? Google the distance and pop the address into your Waze app one morning during peak traffic to get a sense of what the drive will look like—before you apply. Definitely want a larger company with a long-term track record of stability? Look up how many employees they have and investigate if they've gone through any past or recent layoffs.

Websites like Glassdoor.com can be helpful, as long as you take each individual review with a grain of salt. Keep in mind that many of the posts are written by disgruntled ex- (and sometimes current) employees. If you detect a pattern where many of the reviews are stating similar complaints, then it's likely that there is some truth behind them. LinkedIn is another resource for researching companies before applying. See if any of your connections have worked there, and if so, reach out to them and ask for their insight.

NEGATIVE ONLINE REVIEWS

A couple of years ago, I worked with a rapidly grow-ing startup company. They could not hire fast enough and were desperate for help finding qualified people to come on board. Unfortunately, during this same time period, a handful of disgruntled employees left simul-taneously and posted some pretty scathing reviews on Glassdoor.com. This bad press instantly became a very real problem. The company was trying to rehire for the vacant positions in addition to filling the new openings as quickly as possible, but it became very difficult with candidates seeing the negative comments online. Right and left, outstanding candidates were pulling them-selves out of contention for various positions. When my team was brought in, the client said to me, "We have found many great people during our own search efforts but have lost them all. How can we fix this problem?"

For a larger company that had more positive reviews online to counterbalance the negative, or that had been around longer and had built up a positive reputation in the community, a handful of bad reviews might not have been so dramatic. But, in this company's case, it completely crippled their ability to attract and secure talent. Moreover, the negative reviews weren't an accu-rate representation of the workplace. This company was quite a great place to work. They had many happy, loyal employees. But they weren't the ones posting on review sites. The candidates who put too much cre-dence in what they read online would never know the real story.

Always read online reviews with a grain of salt. Remem-ber that people are more likely to post a review when they are disgruntled and have had a bad experience, as opposed to when they are happy. When an employee is happy, they are more apt to go about their daily lives as normal. When an employee is unhappy, they feel tempted to spout off, and often do.

A bad review may be a reflection of someone who was a bad fit from the get-go, as opposed to an indication that something is wrong with the company. One man's trash is another man's treasure, and the same concept applies to jobs. What may be a horrible fit for one person could be a perfect fit for the next. Keep this in mind and do your own diligence so that you don't miss out on a great opportunity for no good reason.

YOU BE THE JUDGE

In terms of negative reviews, consider a romantic relationship analogy: If someone's ex says that a person you're dating is downright awful, that's something that would naturally raise your antennae. But if you're smart, you'll also consider the source—a disgruntled ex. Maybe the two of them were a bad fit for each other from the start, which created a toxic situation. How many couples do you know who were terrible together, but then morph into different (happier, more pleasant) people once they are with new partners who are better suited for them?

We're all bad in someone's story. So much of life is perspective. Likewise, every company is not for every person, but it could be perfect for the next one who comes along. Consider negative opinions, but always evaluate them in proper context. Come to your own conclusions and never rush to judgment.

WHEN YOU THINK IT COULD BE THE RIGHT JOB

Of course, there is only so much information that can be gathered before you formally interview and meet an actual person who can answer your questions. You should, however, be able to dig up enough to get an initial sense of the strength of the fit.

Before you apply for a particular job, you should be feeling confident about two things: first, that you can realistically excel in the role (or at least handle the responsibilities with minimal training); and second, that the position and the employer align with your non-negotiables list. If you can check these two boxes, you should absolutely pursue that position. On the other hand, if it's a stretch, you'll feel it, and it's best to hold back.

One of the key principles I hope you will embrace is that your search should be about quality, not quantity. Let go of the opportunities that just don't fit, because better ones are out there. By no longer expending energy on positions that aren't right for you, you will attract opportunities that will actually improve your life, rather than detract from it.

KEY POINTS IN THIS CHAPTER

Spending time on deep self-reflection before you begin a new search is imperative in attracting the *right* job. Deconstruct your past jobs, preferences, and skillsets thoughtfully.

Trajectory is key. Pick a track that you can stick with as early in your career as possible.

Attack your search from multiple angles. Your network is an especially powerful resource.

Be selective when applying for jobs. Increase your odds of success—and happiness—by only pursuing roles that have the potential to be a good match.

Chapter Two

YOU'VE GOT THIS: HITTING THE SEND BUTTON WITH CONFIDENCE

As with most endeavors in life, planning upfront not only saves time, it also yields better results. Measure twice, cut once. The chapter you are about to read is quite possibly the most important of this entire book. I say that because the "pre-application" phase of the job seeking process is where most candidates fall short. If you have been striking out in your own search, odds are that you have been unknowingly dooming yourself to failure before you even hit "send."

Rather than applying to twenty jobs and receiving no responses, imagine what it would feel like to apply to those same twenty jobs and get five or ten interview requests. Incredible, right? That is our goal here. And, it's a very realistic one, *if* you digest the information herein and apply the advice.

This chapter will show you how to lay the proper groundwork every single time you throw your hat in the ring for a position. You are about to learn how to get noticed by hiring managers consistently, and have a sense of, "They are going to love me!" every time you apply.

THE PURPOSE OF A RESUME

Simply put, the purpose of your resume is to get you a direct conversation with the employer—either in person or over the phone. Best case scenario, your resume converts your candidacy from a lifeless piece of paper to a live person, who is now seen and evaluated as such. You want your resume to lead a hiring manager to conclude, "I want to learn more about this person." If you do get that phone call or email from a potential employer, congratulations! You're in the top 2 percent of applicants. Your resume has done its job.

THE LIFECYCLE OF A RESUME

Before we delve into the insider tips and tricks of how to impress with your resume, let's take a step back and briefly examine what happens to applications once received by employers.

When resumes filter into a company, they might be handled a few different ways. Executive level searches may attract a dozen resumes at most. Due to the nature of the position and the limited number of people out there who are qualified, the employer probably has not done much advertising. Instead, they are relying on internal referral, recruiting agencies, and other similar sources. In situations like this (where the position is senior level and the candidate numbers are low), the resumes are likely to go directly to another executive. The C-suite will have their eyes closely on the hiring process, and will decide which candidates to meet, with or without input from HR.

More typically, employers cast as wide a net as possible. This can result in hundreds of applicants for lower and mid-level positions. That's where HR comes in, buffering the search and making the first round of decisions as to which candidates make it to the interview stage.

Depending on the size of the department, a resume might initially go to an HR associate, who conducts an initial review. That person will separate the incoming resumes into two piles—potential hires and immediate rejections. Depending on the number of applications received (and their quality, or lack thereof), as much as 80 percent to 90 percent might wind up in the "no" pile. The HR associate then hands off the ones that passed the initial test to their HR manager, or a hiring manager overseeing that particular search.

The manager is then tasked with creating a short list of candidates based on specific predetermined criteria. For example, a department head might say something like, "I only want to see candidates who have worked for major Wall Street investment banks and have MBAs from top schools." HR will then sift through the pile of candidates weeding out anyone who does not meet that description. Many excellent candidates will be cut simply because they did not match the mystery preferences of those who will ultimately make the hiring decision.

These selection processes vary from company to company and from position to position.

There is no way to predict how any particular organization processes its applications, but the good news is you don't have to. Whatever the process is, it is; you can't change it. Focus on what you *can* do—which is exactly what we're going to talk about next.

IT'S ALL ABOUT ALIGNMENT

Your ticket to the "yes" pile (the short list of candidates who will be invited to interview) is *relevance*. Your resume must describe your skills and experience in a way that aligns, clearly and logically, with the open position. Relevance is the number one attention-getter. Your grasp of this concept, and your ability to apply it, are vital components of your job search success.

Remember back in English composition class when your teacher would say, "Don't tell me. Show me." The same concept applies with resumes. Hiring managers won't know you're a fit until you *show* them—and you need to do it explicitly. Always keep in mind that a hiring manager or HR professional makes a snap judgment about you in (literally) seconds, so it's important to make the first impression a good one, and fast.

Never assume a person evaluating your resume will read between the lines to decipher how your experience is relevant. The hiring manager doesn't know anything about you. It's not their job to dig for it; it's your job to show them. If someone else out-highlights you in the relevance department, they have a distinct advantage, regardless of who is more qualified.

So, what gives you relevance? Pertinent experience, for one. Also, the places you've worked (competitors of the employer you're applying to?), job titles you've held, and objectives and special skills that parallel the requirements of the open position. Anything you can think of that will cause the hiring manager to say, "Okay, I see the fit. I'll come back to this one. The person is a good match."

One of a hiring manager's biggest pet peeves is having to weed through ridiculous resumes from applicants who are completely unqualified, or totally off base. I've seen entry-level front office staff apply for director-level openings. I salute their ambition, but let's get real—they have no shot at a director title without a few other steps in between. And they know it. I have also seen people with accounting backgrounds apply to work in marketing with zero previous experience, and salespeople apply to lawyer postings without any legal background, or even a JD. I mean, seriously, what were they thinking?!

HR professionals do not appreciate people wasting their time, and they see so many bad resumes on a daily basis that they're practically predisposed to assume that whatever is in front of them is junk because, most of the time, it is.

Now, the unfortunate thing is that *qualified* candidates miss out on opportunities every day because they fail to convey how and why their background is a good match for the position they are applying for. As we discussed in Chapter 1, most organizations spend considerable time writing detailed job postings. The key is to read them carefully, and then make sure that what you're including on your resume relates directly to the open position each time you apply to a job.

> Make sure that what you're including on your resume relates directly to the open position each time you apply to a job.

Does the job description state, "bilingual candidates preferred?" They didn't write that for no reason. So if you speak Spanish, or even did a semester abroad in a Spanish-speaking country, make a point of it.

Here's another example: A job description says that advanced experience in Microsoft Excel is required. Let's say you're well versed in Excel and have used it in your last two jobs, but never thought to highlight that fact on your current resume. Now is the time! And I don't mean casually throw it in somewhere as a subtle afterthought. Emphasize it. Multiple times. Add a bullet point under each employer stating that Excel was a software you used daily (or weekly, or whatever) and describe exactly what projects you used it for. Spell out your capabilities—in detail! Make the effort to show the employer beyond a shadow of a doubt that you are an expert.

By making these thoughtful tweaks, you've just positioned yourself ahead of other applicants who merely listed "Microsoft Excel" in their skills section—or, worse, didn't mention it at all. Do you see the difference? The hiring manager certainly will.

You've heard of the Seven Deadly Sins, right? Gluttony, greed, etc. Well, when it comes to resumes, the Eighth Deadly Sin is omission. One of the most common mistakes candidates make is omission of information. They fail to include their most meaningful experience. I think this happens because it seems so obvious to them, they overlook it.

The best way to avoid that trap is to literally comb through each bullet point of the job description and address each one in your resume. Think about each component listed in the posting—every requirement, every piece of desired experience, every keyword—and then think to yourself, "Does that relate to me?" If the answer is yes, spell it out under the appropriate section or sections of your resume. Then, move on to the next and repeat the process until you have gone through the entire set of requirements and preferences from A to Z.

The more closely a resume aligns with a job description, the better the odds of that candidate being deemed viable. The employer has already told you what they are looking for, in black and white. If you are a good fit for a position, it shouldn't be difficult to illustrate the strength of the match. If you're not a fit, no matter how outstanding your creative writing skills might be, you'll know when you're stretching too far—and so will the hiring manager.

MAKING THE CUT

Think of hiring as a process of elimination because (at least in these early stages) that's exactly what it is. At every step, hiring managers and HR associates are looking for reasons to *reject you.* They're drowning in paper. They need to narrow the field. So the key strategy here is *don't give a hiring manager an easy reason to weed out your application.* It is really that simple.

> Think of hiring as a process of elimination. Don't give a hiring manager an easy reason to weed out your application.

Imagine the scene: An HR associate has a stack of one hundred resumes in front of him, and he's on a tight time constraint. He's been instructed to pass along only the best seven or eight for further review. Anywhere between 50 percent to 75 percent of the resumes are likely to be easy nos. Like we've said, maybe they are way off base, or don't convey the right experience. They'll be tossed in the trash. The remaining, now smaller, stack requires greater discernment. This is where the HR pro will start looking for the most logical ways to whittle the pile down further. Little things become major factors at this stage.

Most candidates have the naive misconception that if you're qualified for a position, you'll automatically get an interview. Not true at all. In reality, your odds of getting an interview largely depend on how well you have illustrated (by tailoring your resume to the job requirements) that you are a match. If you've done this well, it matters far more than your actual qualifications.

Let's take a look at two resumes, both belonging to the same candidate. This is an actual, real-life example of someone that my firm successfully placed last year. The version on the left is her original draft, which she put together on her own. The version on the right is the draft that my team created for her, and which we used when submitting her to our client.

NAME
ADDRESS, PHONE, EMAIL

Hospitality executive specializes in Revenue Management, Strategic Planning, Execution, Online Distribution, Operations, Sales & Marketing

Education
Name of School, Bachelor of Business Administration (June '97)   G.P.A: 3.62/4.00 Double Majors: (1) Marketing (2) Travel Industry Management (TIM) emphasis in Hotel & Restaurant Management Minor: Economics
Dean's List: every semester

Technological Proficiency
Proficiency in various Hotel Property Management Systems (Opera/Fidelio PMS, ORS, OBI Opera Business Intelligence, Revenue Management System - Perform, Stellex, Epiphany, Passkey, Delphi, CLS, OAR-Occupancy Analysis Report; Airline Central Reservation System (Apollo); Restaurant Management Information System; PBX operating system (Meridian GAC-Guest Administration Console and Voicemail)

EXPERIENCE, SKILLS & ACHIEVEMENTS - Hospitality Industry

Area Director of Revenue Management, Company Name, Location (mid-tier and luxury properties totaling 1251 rooms) Dates of Employment

Director of Revenue Management, Property Name, Location, Dates of Employment

Achievements and Responsibilities:
- Consistently exceed year over year revenue performances.
- Conduct presentations quarterly to large audience of over 50 people, public speaking experience.
- Achieved highest total rooms revenue in the history of the hotel for 2 consecutive years.
- Promoted from Revenue Manager to Director of Revenue Management after one year of employment
- Successfully negotiated an unprecedented stop sell room production guarantee
- Created job descriptions for entire department, revamped staffing, created new management position to provide support for additional revenue generated experiences in multi-tier product, cross discipline, cross cultural: hotel, condo; leisure, convention; small, mid, large scale; Asia, US
- Ensure satisfaction of guests, owners, and internal and external customers by aligning the department's performances and operational procedures with the company vision.
- Manage Revenue, Reservation, and Sales functions, supervise managerial staff, Groups and FIT reservations collective bargaining union employees in large size complex properties and resorts
- Ensure service level and satisfaction of guests, owners, internal and external customers by aligning department's performances, operational procedures, with company's vision
- Maximize revenue, maintain and improve market share in a competitive environment, develop strategic goals and implement yield management, maintain pricing integrity, manage channels of distribution effectively in various interactive sources and system interfaces (PMS, RM module, Brand website, Traditional and Online Travel Agencies, Voice-call center and property direct, GDS, Direct Connect, Extranets) and in all markets (Transient, Wholesale, Contracts, Groups, and Owners)
- Provide sound long-term strategic recommendations and short term tactical solutions to property and corporate executives; analyze market trends, competitive set, historical data, booking pace, source of business, segment mix; devise current, historical, forecasting analytical and production reports
- Experience in multi-tier product, cross-discipline, cross-cultural; hotel, condo, leisure, convention, all sizes
- Provide leadership and administrative support to the department, responsible for interviewing, hiring, devising job descriptions, orientation, training, scheduling, payroll, performance evaluations, employee recognition, counseling, disciplinary actions & termination, safety & security, and departmental meetings.

NAME

Professional Experience

Company Name, Location   Dates of Employment
Area Director of Revenue Management
Name of Hotel #1 in portfolio
Name of Hotel #2 in portfolio
Name of Hotel #3 in portfolio

- Drive rooms revenue strategy for multiple properties totaling $70m in annual revenue and 1251 room keys.
- Devise short-term and long-term strategic planning in partnership with Area General Managers, Area Director of Sales & Marketing, Area Financial Controllers, and other senior executives to achieve property revenue goals.
- Consistently exceed year over year revenue performances, including 2014 (4% increase), 2015 (10% increase) and 2016 (7% increase.)
- Oversee individual properties' price-value propositions, business plans, annual rooms revenue, and department expense budgets.
- Conduct weekly strategy meetings.
- Produce 30-60-90-180-360 forecasts by segments, room types, channels, and geographic sources, while maintaining +/-3% forecast accuracy.
- Oversee 8 direct reports, including two managers.
- Maintain 95-100+% STR RevPAR index against local market and comp set.
- Analyze pace and trends for transient, groups, wholesale, and contract markets.
- Brainstorm and implement marketing, PR, and promotional strategies for new revenue opportunities.
- Present to owners and corporate executives on a weekly, monthly, and quarterly basis.

Company Name, Location   Dates of Employment
Director of Revenue Management
Name of Hotel

- Drove rooms revenue strategy for a single luxury property totaling $20M in annual revenue and 327 room keys.
- Maximized revenue, maintained and improved market share in a competitive market, developed strategic goals, implemented yield management, and maintained pricing integrity.
- Analyzed market trends, competitive set, historical data, booking pace, and sources of business.
- Achieved highest total rooms revenue in the history of the hotel for 2 consecutive years.
- Promoted from Revenue Manager to DORM after only 1 year of employment.
- Successfully negotiated an unprecedented stop-sell, room production guarantee.
- Created job descriptions for the entire department, revamped staffing, and created a new position to provide support and additional revenue generation.

EDUCATION & TECHNOLOGICAL PROFICIENCIES

BA, Business Administration, Name of School   *Location*

Well-versed in Opera, SalesPro, CI/TY, Delphi, SynXis, Microsoft Office Suite

CERTIFICATIONS & AWARDS

Certified Revenue Management Executive (CRME), Date
Revenue Management Professional of the Year, Company, Date

The difference is dramatic, isn't it? At first glance, they look as if they belong to two completely different people. But in fact, both versions describe the same person and career, just presented differently. The original draft is poorly formatted, convoluted, unfocused, bloated, and hard to follow. The second version is easy to read, pleasing to the eye, highly targeted, specific, streamlined, relevant to the job, and contains no filler or fluff.

Again—same exact candidate, totally different presentation on paper. This is a perfect example of someone who was the right fit for a position, but would never have even gotten to the interview phase without our help repackaging her experience. The overhaul on this resume made all the difference between the candidate getting hired versus being overlooked. This is big stuff!

Let's delve a little deeper into how and why fluff can hurt you. Let's say you work in sales, but you organized a major corporate event that went flawlessly and you received a lot of praise and good press. You put it on your resume. Next time you go to apply for a sales job, the person reviewing the documents is likely to question your goals. They might think, "Wow, that's really impressive. Maybe event planning is where this person's heart really is? I'm not sure if we should hire her in this sales role." At the very least, it's an unnecessary distraction.

This is why you must resist the urge to list everything you've ever done on your resume. I know, I know, you're proud that you were captain of the swim team in high school, joined a sorority in college, and have volunteered on a few political campaigns. As impressive as all that may be, most of the time it's better to leave miscellaneous details out and stick to specific aspects of your experience that are directly relevant to the position you're applying for. Overkill on a resume is like a longwinded answer and will invite the hiring manager to tune out. Also, *the more content you include, the more ammo you give the reviewer to zero in on something they don't like* that could ultimately rule you out.

DON'T BE A CLICHÉ

Canned phrases like, "I'm detail oriented," and "I'm a team player," may apply to you, but they are painfully overused on resumes. Most hiring managers completely disregard these terms because they are empty and cliché. They won't do you any favors or help you to stand out. In fact, they'll just cause you to blend in with competition. Be more creative to differentiate yourself from the pack.

FORMATTING MATTERS (AND, YES, SO DOES SIZE)

Candidates constantly ask me what resume format is most effective. While HR professionals all have their preferences, you can never go wrong with a clean, concise, easy-to-follow template. No frills, no pictures, no colored text, no fancy fonts. No emojis. Just clean and simple. Boring, maybe. But effective. Let the content speak for itself.

As far as length goes, always keep it to two pages or less.

Anything beyond that will probably not be read, and you'll run the risk of annoying the person reviewing it. I've heard countless employers say that if a candidate can't communicate their experience clearly on two pages or less, it's a red flag. Why? Because it's an indication that the person isn't a clear thinker or succinct communicator. Certainly not a first impression that presents someone as an ideal potential employee.

FLUFF DOESN'T FLY

Just as it's important to include aspects of your background that are relevant to a position, you also must take the time to weed out any details that are irrelevant. Include content that shows you are a match for the position and *eliminate everything else*. Focused and simple is the name of the game.

> Include content that shows you are a match for the position and *eliminate everything else*. Focused and simple is the name of the game.

That being said, there are exceptions. Always view your content through the lens of common sense. Listing your high school sports accomplishments may be ridiculous when you are forty years old and applying for a new position in finance, but it may actually be relevant if you are applying to a company whose mission revolves around sports, or if you're fresh out of college and the job description states they want someone with leadership experience. By all means, in those scenarios, mention you were captain of the cross-country team and won a few gold medals.

Do you see how this works? The key is evaluating each opportunity individually and thinking logically about what is applicable to the job. You'll always know the answer about what to include and what not to if you read the job description thoughtfully and just be smart about it.

Why is keeping your resume short and sweet so important? Because when you don't do it, you're essentially asking the reviewer to spend their precious time *finding* your relevant experience. That's a dangerous tactic. Plus, eventually, your broad and unfocused resume will come up against one that is highly specialized and targeted for the job. Which candidate do you think the hiring manager will be more excited to invite for an interview?

It blows many peoples' minds to know that the applicant with the best, most specialized resume isn't necessarily the better candidate for the job. But on paper (which is literally all that matters at this point), they look far more attractive.

> The applicant with the best, most specialized resume isn't necessarily the better candidate for the job. But on paper (which is literally all that matters at this point), they look far more attractive.

Be intentional about all of your content. Be hyperaware of every single word on the page. Is it there for a reason? Trim extra words and phrases. Don't just fill boxes because they're included in a random resume template. The more miscellaneous content you include, you're just opening yourself up for a hiring manager to say, "We don't need those skills," or "I don't like that," and "I have other candidates here who look like a better fit."

Always keep thinking to yourself, "simple and relevant." It is always the best strategy, ten times out of ten. I know it may make you feel one dimensional, or like you are leaving out aspects of what makes you so interesting, and that can be frustrating. But remember, you're not trying to dazzle HR (yet). For now, you're just trying to give them confidence that you can do the job, while avoiding anything that will turn them off. At this stage, you just want to get them interested on paper. They will see you in three dimensions soon enough.

JOB TITLES

A mismatched job title can cause your resume to be dismissed instantly. Say, for instance, you're applying for a director of finance position, but the titles on your resume are different—VP of finance, assistant controller, or something similar. Some hiring managers won't read another word. They immediately think, "I have fifty other candidates here who have director of finance on their resume. Why would I look at someone who doesn't?"

Of course, it's never a good idea to lie and masquerade as something you're not, but oftentimes there's a middle ground. Let's say you work in the hospitality industry as an on-property controller, which is essentially synonymous to the position titled director of finance. It just so happens that your property uses different terminology than your potential new employer. In this circumstance, I would recommend changing your title to director of finance instead of controller. It will help you make it into the "yes" pile, while still representing yourself in a fair and accurate way. As long as you do have the proper experience, this is fair game.

Be really conscious of titles, because they are one of the very first aspects of a resume that screeners tune into. Perfectly qualified applicants are rejected every day because of mismatched titles on their resume.

Here's another example: There are administrative professionals out there doing executive assistant work under the title of administrative assistant. They are working one-on-one, supporting executives or directors, and yet their title does not reflect their actual experience. I would never suggest that a candidate exaggerate, like call themselves a director of finance when they were really an assistant director; I hope that goes without saying. But if your title has been administrative assistant and you have been doing the work of an executive assistant, a tweak in the title is not inappropriate if it does a better job of telling the true story. If a person in this situation were applying to an EA job, they should change the title accordingly. Likewise, if they were applying to postings titled administrative assistant, they should leave their title as is—administrative assistant.

With regard to past employment, dates should always be included. And be specific—list the month and the year. If you only include years, it is a red flag. The hiring manager will immediately question if you are being vague to disguise gaps, or to hide the fact that "2017–2018" really meant a three-month stint from December of 2017 to March of 2018. Vagueness will raise suspicion that you are hiding something.

MATCH YOUR OBJECTIVE (!!!)

This is huge. The objective statement you include on your resume can literally make or break you—no matter how otherwise qualified you are. I have seen countless candi-

THE DREADED FREELANCE YEARS

It is hard to sell most employers on candidates who have held freelance gigs. The stereotypical concerns are that freelancers can't work for other people, that they're too independent to take direction from a "boss," and that they are a flight risk—they like variety and will get bored staying in one place for too long. Accurate or not, these are the perceptions.

If you have been freelancing for a number of years, fear not, there are some strategic ways to frame that experience in the best possible light. Let's say you've been an independent contractor doing social media work for five years. List that five-year period as one section of your resume. Label it "social media consultant," to illustrate that you've been consulting for five years doing consistent work. Under that header, list a few of your clients, what you've done for them, and the results you've achieved. Describe the specifics of projects you've worked on that might be relevant to your next employer. Now, suddenly you present as someone who has a five-year tenure as a consultant working for a handful of companies consistently, as opposed to someone who job hopped four times in five years—big difference!

dates apply for jobs and be tossed in the "no" pile because their objective doesn't match the position.

Given its placement at the top of the page, your objective is the very first thing any hiring manager or recruiter is likely to zero in on. Even if your background is a strong match for the open role and you've done a great job showing relevance throughout the body of your resume, a contrary or mismatched objective will derail your candidacy every time.

Yes, it is true that you can't always predict exactly what will go over well and what won't. But if you use common sense based on the information you do have, you'll be right the vast majority of the time.

If you ever find yourself struggling to come up with just the right objective, or tweaking it appropriately, leave it off. You're always better off not having one at all than including one that doesn't fit. Don't allow your first impression to be an instant disqualifier.

THEY KNOW WHERE YOU LIVE (OR DO THEY?)

If you list a home address on your resume that is in a different geographic location than the job opening, your application will likely wind up in the trash. For example, if you are applying for jobs in New York, but your resume indicates that you live in Florida, you'll be fast-tracked to the "no" pile. Companies prefer to hire local whenever possible, especially for lower to mid-level positions. Why deal with relocating someone, and the risks associated with that, when they don't have to?

It's important to be aware of this, in case you ever find yourself in the process of moving. Maybe you have

HOW AN OBJECTIVE CAN ELIMINATE YOU

Here's an example of how a written objective can eliminate a candidate through no fault of their own. Certain jobs are static, meaning there's really no path for growth. Let's say, for example, a company has an IT department of three people—two associates and a manager. There could be growth opportunity for an associate to eventually rise to manager level, but after that the growth potential is maxed out (manager is the highest level position that exists in that department).

Now let's say you work in HR at that same company, and the IT manager position is open. You have been tasked with sifting through the resumes and establishing the short list. Suddenly you come across a resume with an objective that states something like, "Skilled IT professional looking for continued growth, and an environment where I can further develop my leadership abilities." (This is an actual, real-life example.) Chances are, this candidate has just blown it, especially if the field is competitive. Why? They have just expressed in black and white that they are looking for upward mobility, and an opportunity to manage a larger team. That's all admirable, but it's not in alignment with what the company can offer. Any savvy HR professional will pick up on that. At best, they'll see it as a red flag. At worst, they'll immediately disregard the candidate altogether. Always make sure that your objective aligns with the role you are applying for. Don't raise a red flag unnecessarily.

already made the decision to relocate to New York, but you're currently looking at real estate (or waiting until you have a job nailed down before you commit to an actual apartment). You have every intention of changing cities but don't have a formal address just yet. Unless you make your relocation plans crystal clear on your application, the hiring manager is going to say, "This person has a great background, but she's not local. On to the next." To prevent this from happening, always list your *new* city as your location, even if you do not yet have a specific home address. In the contact information section of your resume, just list your cell number, email address, and "New York, NY."

AVOID THE HARD SELL

You already know to remove anything, *everything,* that is not directly relevant to the position. You've combed through every bullet point, confirming that every word and sentence has a purpose. Now what? Is there anything else to filter out? Yes.

Avoid the hard sell. The best resumes are matter of fact. They convey, "This is where I've worked. This is what I've done." They communicate pertinent information succinctly. They do not oversell or stress the same content over and over again.

If you're overselling your accomplishments, they may come across as inauthentic. A resume that is too "salesy" will cause the person reviewing your documents to wonder if maybe you haven't been as successful as you're projecting. It's okay to cite meaningful numbers. If you increased sales by a certain percentage, say so. But skip the superlatives, the quotes from your boss about how great you are, and so on. Communicate your experience and results and leave it at that.

Here's a litmus test to tell what's appropriate: Would you state your resume bullets in conversation? If they sound over the top and braggadocios when spoken, chances are they'll be a turnoff on paper, too. When it comes to stating information on resumes, facts go a long way. In a lineup of resumes, you want yours to be the cleanest and most fact filled, not boastful or over the top.

> In a lineup of resumes, you want yours to be the cleanest and most fact filled, not boastful or over the top.

DON'T BE *THAT GUY*

Desperation has a cost. If you are applying for every position at a particular company, basically spamming the HR team, they're *not* going to think, "Wow, this person is really motivated and wants to work here. Let's give him an interview." Instead, their reaction will be, "Who is this guy? Why won't he leave us alone?" You may even look crazy after a while, to the point where HR looks at your resume and thinks, "Oh, no. Not *him* again."

It's also unwise to have your resume floating around just

anywhere. For one thing, if your employer catches wind that you're actively looking, that's obviously not good for you. It's amazing how many people have their resume just sitting on places like Indeed or Monster for anyone to see. If you think an HR person in your own company isn't scouring those same websites, you're mistaken. I have also heard clients say that they won't hire candidates who perpetually post their resume publicly. Why? Because nobody wants to employ someone who is always looking for the next best thing. Employers think, "If we hire this girl, who's to say she'll be loyal to us? She's clearly the type of person who is always open to what else is out there." True or not, that's the perception. Be discreet.

It's unwise to have your resume floating around just anywhere. If you think an HR professional in your own company isn't scouring the same websites, you're mistaken.

On the other hand, folks who are unemployed or just out of school and looking for work can benefit from that kind of broad visibility, without any downside. If you fall into either of these categories (or a similar one), exposure is good for you. When unemployed, the more places your resume is posted, the better—so feel free to post away. But once you find a new position, take your resume down. Don't leave your information lingering out in space after you've been hired.

BE HONEST

Sadly, many people lie on their resumes. I say don't do it for a myriad of reasons, the most obvious of which is that it's just wrong. A dear friend of mine always says, "The truth is like a cork," meaning, the truth always comes to the surface eventually. It is so true. If you lie, it won't hold up for long. Eventually someone will find out. You might make it a week into the interview process, or even six months on the job, but eventually your dishonesty will backfire, sometimes irreparably.

The best, smartest job seekers get a lot further by figuring out an intelligent way to present the truth. We've all made mistakes or had those little blips we wish we could do over. We're human. And honestly, hiring managers understand that and are often more empathetic than you might think. What they absolutely despise is being lied to.

So, if there is an aspect of your professional past that you would like to de-emphasize, (perhaps a gap in employment, or the fact that you've job hopped a couple of times recently due to circumstances beyond your control), nine times out of ten, you can get by that with a hiring manager by simply being upfront about it and presenting a story that makes logical sense.

Did you take a year off from work because you were taking care of a sick family member? Did you change jobs three times in five years because the companies you worked for went through ownership changes that forced massive layoffs? Explain this. If you don't, the hiring manager will question if you are flaky or lazy, when in reality you are anything but. Again, they won't know unless you tell them. These situations won't be held against you if you get out ahead of them in an honest and confident way.

The freelance work situation we discussed earlier in this chapter is another good example. The past is what it is, but it's also yours to repackage. You have the power to shape your freelance experience into a picture that looks either entrepreneurial or unstable. One says, "Look how many clients I built up, and all the relevant projects I worked on." The other says, "I just kind of floated around and took what came." Identical experience, packaged to look and sound like two entirely different candidates. Which person would you hire?

EDUCATION

College seniors often wonder if they should include their GPA or their coursework on their resume. I know most entry-level professionals won't want to hear this, but the truth is, nobody cares. Employers will not select or reject you over the courses you took, the grades you earned, or the specific major you declared.

Now, in certain situations your major could be meaningful; for example, if a company needs an employee with a specific degree, like accounting or psychology. Otherwise, once you're a couple of years out of school, all a hiring manager cares about is: A) whether or not you graduated and B) any real-world work experience you've had since then. And the latter weighs far more heavily. Your college degree is essentially a check-the-box; "Does this person have a college degree? Okay, great." Any other details about your coursework and grades are generally irrelevant.

The Education section of your resume should look the same, regardless of your age. Plain and simple, just list your school(s) and degree(s). Inclusion of the year you graduated is at your discretion. Some employers like to see it; however, be aware that including it will enable them to guess at your age, and pretty accurately. "Oh, he graduated in 2015? That was three years ago, which means he's probably 25." Maybe this isn't a big deal to you, but if you're really young or nearing retirement where the date might be a distraction, you're probably wise to leave it off.

Age discrimination is a real thing. Yes, I know it's illegal. But age is factored into hiring decisions all the time. I have heard employers say that they will only consider women past child-bearing years, because they don't want to deal with the disruption of maternity leaves. I have also heard employers say that they won't consider any candidate over the age of 60, because the person will inevitably retire in a few years. These scenarios happen every day. For this reason alone, I recommend that you leave the year of your graduation off your resume. It goes back to not giving hiring managers any easy reason to rule you out before they have met you in person.

What if you went to college and completed a couple of years, but did not graduate? Leave that information off your resume. Unless you have an actual degree, the fact that you completed some college coursework is irrelevant to most employers. Also, including that information opens you up to being asked in an interview, "When did you obtain your degree?" And, you'll say, "Oh, I don't have one. I didn't graduate." Neither of you will be happy at that point that you included college on your resume.

Athletics and leadership positions have a longer shelf life. I have worked with a handful of companies who hire entry-level candidates fresh out of college, and they really like seeing things like team sports. They feel this type of activity shows initiative and competitive spirit, traits that are especially attractive in sales roles. These employers want to know you did more than sit in a classroom for four years. Internships, sports, social clubs, any pursuits outside of coursework (especially if you've held a leadership position) are definitely helpful to include.

But here's the key: These things matter for a handful of years after college, at most. Certainly by the time you're thirty, no one cares about much other than your actual work experience. So within a few years after graduation, I recommend removing the college extracurriculars, because they will start to look like filler. You want to present in a way that will make the reviewer think, "Wow, this person seems solid and has held a serious job for three years." As opposed to, "This person just graduated from college not long ago. She won't have the maturity we need." How you position yourself makes an enormous difference.

If you're still within five years of graduating, those activities are best placed in the Education section. You could add another bullet point such as, "leadership experience." List your extracurricular roles and responsibilities, but keep them brief and to the point. Again, the more you emphasize the college years, the younger and greener you will seem, and that is unlikely to do you any favors.

MULTIPLE RESUMES?

Depending on your situation, it may make sense for you to have two versions of your resume that illustrate your background from different angles. If you've accumulated two distinctly separate or complementary skillsets in your career, you should absolutely have two resumes, each highlighting one side of your experience. You would then submit whichever version is most appropriate each time you apply to a new position. If you go this route, you'll still want to do a quick comb through and double-check for relevance each time you apply. But having two versions will give you a strong template to start from in either scenario.

Here is another real-life example. The following resumes belong to another candidate we have represented in the past. This person has both administrative and HR experience in her background, and created two different resumes (one to emphasize each). Amazing that they both accurately represent the same person, right? But they do!

NAME

Street • City, State Zip
email • phone

ADMINISTRATIVE ASSISTANT

Experienced administrative professional with direct experience supporting C-level executives and management teams.

PROFESSIONAL EXPERIENCE

Company Name
Company description, location   Dates of Employment
Administrative Assistant

- Provide administrative support to 2 C-level staff and 3 department heads.
- Schedule appointments as directed. Manage and maintain Outlook calendars and contacts.
- Maintain up-to-date to-do list for the CEO, and ensure that tasks are completed in a timely manner.
- Maintain all employee files, both paper and electronic.
- Draft correspondence, both hand-written and e-mail.
- Book travel arrangements, including flights, hotels, and rental cars. Produced and distributed detailed itineraries prior to each trip.
- Assemble new hire packets and other documents needed for various on-site and off-site meetings.
- Answer phones and take detailed messages.
- Handle sensitive information with the utmost confidentiality.

Company Name
Company description, location   Dates of Employment
Administrative Assistant

- Provided administrative support to a busy office of 35 employees.
- Drafted formal letters, contracts, emails, and other documents.
- Assisted in the writing of various office policies and procedures.
- Booked travel arrangements, including flights, hotels, and rental cars. Produced and distributed detailed itineraries prior to each trip.
- Performed research in support of senior level staff projects as delegated.
- Created onboarding packets for new hires.
- Tracked employee hours and vacation time.
- Ordered all office supplies and tracked inventory.

EDUCATION AND CREDENTIALS

- **BA, Liberal Studies** – Name of College

TECHNICAL PROFICIENCIES

Microsoft Office Suite (Word, Excel, Outlook, PowerPoint) & QuickBooks

HUMAN RESOURCES GENERALIST

Energetic, quality-focused Human Resources professional with extensive experience in employee relations, benefits administration, HRIS, and project management. A trusted resource to senior leadership teams.

PROFESSIONAL EXPERIENCE

Company Name
Company description, location   Dates of Employment
Human Resources Generalist

- Perform all human resources functions, including recruitment, onboarding of new hires, benefits administration and research, employee relations, and payroll.
- Manage all employee files, including creation of an HR information database.
- Oversee all HR functions for four office locations, with 120 employees in total.
- Serve as key resource for owner and employees in interpreting employment laws and compliance issues.
- Create and deliver trainings related to diversity, safety, and sexual harassment for all staff.
- Investigate employee claims and concerns, and lead response and resolution as appropriate.
- Assist in the production of HRIS and financial reports.

Company Name
Company description, location   Dates of Employment
Human Resources Assistant

- Assisted in the writing and consistent implementation of all human resources functions, policies, and procedures.
- Researched benefit costs and advantages of different types of medical coverage to reduce expense.
- Assisted in the hiring process, including screening candidates and conducting first round interviews.
- Created onboarding packets for new hires, and drafted formal offer letters.
- Tracked employee hours and vacation time.
- Assisted in the processing of biweekly payroll.

EDUCATION AND CREDENTIALS

- **BA, Liberal Studies** – Name of College
- Professional of Human Resources (PHR) certification, Date
- Member, Society for Human Resource Management (SHRM), Date

TECHNICAL PROFICIENCIES

HRIS, PeopleSoft, Viewpoint Vista, ADP, Oracle, QuickBooks, and Microsoft Office Suite

As you can see, it is possible to look like two entirely different candidates on paper, while still conveying your experience in an honest way. This particular person saw an immediate uptick in the number of application responses she received once she began applying the two resumes strategy. Taking the time to do this can be a game changer for many candidates. Are you one of them?

WHAT ABOUT MORE THAN TWO VERSIONS?

Theoretically, a custom version of your resume could be created every single time you apply. In a perfect world, you'd create as many variations as you possibly can without going completely insane. Why? Because each job is unique and will require a slightly different resume to really stand out.

I know it's a pain. I know it is a lot of work. But this is the kind of effort that will set you apart from the other candidates vying for the jobs you want and deserve. Besides, if you're heeding my advice and applying to jobs selectively, tweaking the different versions of your resume shouldn't be as labor intensive as it sounds.

If the two-resume strategy doesn't apply to you and your experience, a good hack is to have one "base resume" that you customize. Save a document on your computer that includes absolutely everything you have ever done that you can possibly think to include. Each time you apply for a job, refer back to the base draft. Start pulling all relevant content point by point from the base copy and placing it into a new document, while leaving the rest behind. When you're done, you'll have a customized resume geared to the job you're applying for. That's the best method. It enables you to have all of your information stored in one place, and create as many unique versions necessary, with minimal effort.

NEED A COVER LETTER?

sonal opinion is that most of the time you are better
including a cover letter. Why? Because it is just one
more aspect of your application that the reviewer can,
and will, use to knock you out of the running. Remember,
the reviewer is looking for any excuse to eliminate you.

If your resume is great, but something glaring is caught
on the cover letter that the reviewer doesn't like, you're
toast. My advice on this is simple: If a company specifically requires a cover letter, include one. Otherwise, don't.

Cover letters are risky due to the sheer amount of content.
Any single sentence you write is up for scrutiny and could
ruin your chances of getting the job. Almost anything
could cause the hiring manager to say, "Oh, I don't like
that," or, "This person won't be a good fit for our opening."

Beyond the potential ammunition for exclusion, your
writing will be dissected. Things like poor grammar,
punctuation, spelling, and word choice can instantly put
you in a bad light. If a position requires a tremendous
amount of detail orientation, the hiring manager will be
combing that cover letter line by line for mistakes. If they
catch any, it's all too easy for them to justify tossing your
application to the side, saying, "See, this person doesn't
have what it takes to succeed in this role; they didn't even
catch the errors in their own cover letter."

A candidate with a perfectly written cover letter, or someone who doesn't submit one at all, will prevail over someone who submits a bad one. Again, that doesn't mean that candidate is a better fit for the position, but it does mean they've done a better job of presenting themselves. And as you know by now, that has a tremendous impact on who gets hired.

While a perfect cover letter is your best-case scenario, most people won't put in the effort required to craft anything better than mediocre. In cases where employers "strongly encourage" a cover letter, put in the time to write a really stellar letter, and have a detail-oriented friend comb it for mistakes. Having a fresh set of eyes on your document from someone you trust can be extremely helpful.

CANNED VS. ORIGINAL

Never use a canned cover letter pulled off the internet. Generic letters are almost an insult to the person reading them, because they signify that you didn't care enough about the position to craft something personalized and original. Pepper in personal anecdotes. Be specific. Reference pieces of the job description to let HR know (or at least feel like) you wrote the letter just for them. If you manage to convey sincere interest and include personal touches while avoiding technical mistakes (spelling, grammar, etc.), your letter will be a home run.

SUPPLEMENTAL MATERIALS

What about attaching additional documents to your application? Separate documents sometimes add value. Maybe you work in the construction industry and want to highlight some of your key building projects. Absolutely fine. Compile a concise, well-formatted list and include it as a separate document. It should have a clear, descriptive title (e.g., "Projects List") and should be no more than one page. Done right, and with fully relevant content, this may actually go a long way toward differentiating you from other candidates. Even so, HR folks still emphasize the resume; keep in mind that sparkling supplementary documents will only do you so much good if your resume is irrelevant or poorly done.

In creative professions like web or graphic design, it's common to see portfolio links on the resume. These little touches can be effective in the proper circumstances. Know what is considered customary for your particular industry and act accordingly. Just make sure the additional content does not distract from a reviewer's ability to capture the most important content in a matter of seconds. The information of utmost relevance should always be the most obvious on the page.

WHAT ABOUT PHOTOS?

Do not include a photo of yourself on your resume. Do include one on your LinkedIn page.

Here's another hiring truth that most people in the industry will never admit: candidates are ruled out over physical appearance *all the time*. Let's say, for example, that a company is looking for a catering sales manager at their private club or hotel. It is a very client-facing position, and they need someone who will represent their company with the utmost sophistication amidst an elite customer demographic. Their vision of the ideal candidate is someone polished and attractive, who will show up to work every day smartly dressed and exceptionally well groomed.

If a candidate applies for this position and they look sloppy in their LinkedIn photo, I promise you they will wind up in the "no" pile in a matter of seconds, regardless of the strength of their qualifications.

The HR professionals filtering out resumes and reviewing your photos online are people, too, and pictures are susceptible to their particular likes, dislikes, and biases. A clean resume with no pictures eliminates distraction. So does a LinkedIn photo of quality that represents you as a well-dressed, clean-cut professional. It is important to note here that employers aren't assessing how "attractive" someone is; rather, they are judging the level of professionalism, dress, and polish.

We've already discussed how your goal at this stage is to get a face-to-face interview, where you'll have the opportunity to truly show the hiring team who you are. Part of avoiding triggering any bias in the initial filtering process is having appropriate photos. Be thoughtful about your LinkedIn profile photo in particular. It is likely the first visual representation of you that a potential employer will see. And first impressions matter.

LINKEDIN AND ATTRACTING RECRUITERS

LinkedIn is another place where people tend to describe everything they've ever done. A better strategy is to keep it simple on LinkedIn, just like on your resume. Your page needs to have enough information to show that you are a real person, validate your resume, and perhaps provide some additional snippets that shed light on who you are.

Did you write an industry-related article that you are really proud of? Is there a particular charitable organization that you are involved with? This type of content can bring warmth and depth to you as a candidate, and the way in which you are perceived. I do recommend peppering some in, while being cautious not to overshadow your professional experience.

Your profile should be concise enough that it is clean and easy to read, but still robust enough that you can be found in search results (assuming that you want to be!)

LinkedIn is one of the most popular tools that internal and external recruiters use to source candidates, and they do so largely by using filters. They enter through special, upgraded employer or recruiter accounts, and LinkedIn works just like a search engine.

Search criteria might include geographic location, position title, software proficiencies, special skills, and even specific past or present employers. When my recruiting team runs a search, we're thinking through what our client needs and wants in a candidate. Then, we come up with a strategic list of what to search for in order to unearth those candidates. We run the search, and every LinkedIn candidate that matches our criteria, in order of relevance, pops up for review.

Keywords come into play here, in a big way. Recruiters often search by catchwords and jargon that are common in certain industries. In hospitality, keywords might be property qualifiers like "Four Diamond," "Five Star," or "boutique property." In order to appear in the recruiter's search result, the words in your profile must match the terms that they are searching. The more times they appear, the higher up in the search result you'll be.

If you want to be found by recruiters, look at your profile through their eyes. Think to yourself, "If someone were searching for a candidate like me, what criteria would they use? Does that reflect the content that is in my profile?" If the answer is no, make the necessary adjustments.

Recruiters are not necessarily looking only for candidates who have flagged themselves as open to job opportunities. They're searching everyone with a LinkedIn profile who meets the criteria that the employer is looking for. It is in their best interest to cast a wide net, because the more qualified candidates in the pipeline, the better the employer's chance of successfully filling the position. So, recruiters sift through long lists, sometimes even hundreds deep. That's round one.

From there, the human element kicks in. Round two involves reading the profiles in more detail, similar to the way resumes are reviewed. The recruiter is looking at professional qualifications, employers, photos, areas of expertise, and so on. Based on the content in the profiles, the recruiter would then decide which potential candidates are still a fit, versus who should be ruled out. Those who are interesting enough to be worth deeper exploration are then placed on the recruiter's short list.

Once the short list has been established, recruiters will then begin reaching out to candidates. Every recruiter's process is unique. Oftentimes they will send a connection request first, because that's how a LinkedIn member's contact information (such as phone number or email) becomes visible to them. If you find yourself on the receiving end of a connection request or InMail message from a recruiter, that is an outstanding position to be in if you are open to a new opportunity.

The savvy recruiters, however, will skip that step because they'll have other means of reaching you. They probably invest in one of the many resources out there that provide ways of tracking down candidates' contact information. Why? Because it enables them to get in contact much faster. Rather than waiting for a candidate to accept their connection request or reply to their InMail, they can take control of the process by just picking up the phone and calling you.

If that doesn't work, they'll find your email address. If *that* doesn't work, there's always Facebook or other social media platforms. You get the idea. The most persistent and skilled headhunters will always find a way to reach the candidates they have their eye on.

Once in touch, they might say something like, "Hi, I'm working with a confidential client to fill a particular opening, and I believe you could be a strong fit because of X, Y, and Z. Are you open to a conversation? I'd like to learn more about your background, and I can give you more information about the position as well."

The more senior level the position, the more extensive the vetting process. And that vetting can go both ways. The smartest candidates I have worked with over the years have insisted on doing their homework on me and my firm before talking further. I always respect this, because it shows me that the person is thoughtful, and taking the process seriously.

Their diligence helps build trust on both sides of the equation. Once they decide to move forward, I know that this person and I have already established a solid foundation. This will help our working relationship, and hopefully the end result (ideally, a successful placement).

If you are ever lucky enough to be on the receiving end of a call from a recruiter or employer, congratulations. It means that they already have a sincere interest in you. If they are good, they're probably correct that you have high potential to be a fit for the open role. At the very least, there is certainly enough meat there to explore. Think of it this way: You've just bypassed the entire craziness of the resume submission process, finger-crossing, and waiting. The recruiter found you, and they're telling you that you're a good candidate. It's a satisfying (and exciting!) place to be.

If a recruiter contacts you and you're even *remotely* interested in exploring new opportunities, you should absolutely take these out-of-the-blue communications very seriously. It may seem odd, almost like spam, but I assure you, these opportunities are typically legit, assuming the employment agency is reputable.

Of course, there are some unscrupulous, unprofessional recruiters out there. Every industry has its share of folks who are great at what they do, and those who make us cringe. Remember, however, it's in a recruiter's own best interest to place people. They make their money when they actually fill openings, so they literally can't afford to waste their time on candidates that don't fit the bill.

While it's possible they may make a bad judgment call every now and then, I stand by this advice: when a recruiter contacts you via LinkedIn or some other means, take the opportunity seriously. The recruiter has already done some degree of diligence and is contacting you for a reason.

OTHER SOCIAL MEDIA

Social accounts matter more than you might think. Some candidates say, "My Instagram is personal. My Facebook is my private life. No employer should care or judge me based on what I post." Well, yes and no. While it's technically true that social accounts are personal, they are still a reflection of you as a person, your values, and how you conduct yourself. In the eyes of employers, those are clues as to what type of employee you will be.

> While it's technically true that social accounts are personal, they are still a reflection of you as a person, your values, and how you conduct yourself. In the eyes of employers, those are clues as to what type of employee you will be.

The importance of social media may increase based on the individual employer, the seniority of a position, or how client-facing a role will be. But even for entry-level professionals, your online presence matters. If you are being considered for a brand ambassador position at a company that specializes in luxury products, the hiring manager is not going to be thrilled if they check your Facebook page and see you getting blackout drunk every weekend or posting highly controversial memes on a regular basis.

You may not feel it is anyone's business what you do on your own time outside of work, but it becomes the employer's business if your weekend antics, political views, and so on are in full public view and in conflict with the brand that you could potentially be representing. Sometimes it's not even the behavior itself that turns hiring managers off, but it's the fact that you're choosing to post about it. There's a way to live your life the way you want to and be discreet about it. Not everything you think and do needs to be posted online.

Be authentic and "do you," but always consider the image you're putting out there. Does it align with the job you want, or does it conflict? Be smart about what you put on social media, especially during a job search. Regardless of your age or your career path, you are building a personal brand with every single piece of content that you put out there. And employers have every right to investigate and have a judgment about that personal brand.

> Be authentic and "do you," but always consider the image you're putting out there. Does it align with the job you want, or does it conflict?

PRIVATE PROFILES

By this point you might be thinking, "Okay, so if I don't want employers scrutinizing my social media, that's an easy fix—I'll just set my accounts to private."

Bad idea.

When recruiters or hiring managers encounter social profiles that are set to private, they are apt to wonder, "What is this person hiding? Why aren't they transparent?"

Ironically, private profiles are almost more of a red flag because they hide that human piece of the puzzle.

If an employer is looking you up on social media, they want to know more about you. This is an opportunity for you to win them over. Why ruin that chance by blocking them from seeing who you are in "real life?" Stay away from false names, too. I know it is a growing trend for people to post their content under secret names that only their friends know. Recruiters much prefer to deal with people who are straightforward, as opposed to those who take a shady approach to social media (or, frankly, to any other aspect of who they are and how they present). Keep your profiles public, and just be thoughtful about what you post.

For the sake of the long-term employee-employer relationship, make this awareness a habit so that you are consistent before and during employment. Once you are in the door of a company, everyone should see the same version of you that they grew to genuinely like during the interview process.

It's kind of like losing weight. In the long run, are you doing yourself a favor by crash dieting to get a quick result, or are you better off making healthy lifestyle changes and being consistent about it? We all know the answer. Same concept applies here.

BEING PREPARED FOR THE PHONE CALL

Always include a phone number on your application materials. Ideally, it should be a personal cell that will be answered by you and only you (no home or office numbers). It is off-putting to a hiring manager when their call is answered by children, a spouse, a roommate, or a coworker—basically, anyone other than the candidate.

Also keep in mind that any delay in response on your part will indicate a lack of interest. Be sure to use a number with reliable voicemail that you monitor carefully and return messages promptly. Better yet, pick up the phone when it rings.

When someone calls you in response to your application, they are intent on making contact. This is a big deal, as it is a segue into being taken seriously as a candidate. Starting that human interaction off on the right foot is crucial, and the first impression that you give over the phone will make or break it.

Record a professional voicemail greeting that represents you well. Yes, you can be ruled out for certain positions based on what you sound like over your voicemail. For instance, if a company is hiring for a sales position, they are looking for candidates who are energetic, charismatic, upbeat, and friendly. Particularly if the position involves phone sales, you can bet that HR is going to be paying special attention to how candidates project over the phone, whether live or on voicemail. If the recruiter comes across a voicemail greeting that is low energy and lacking warmth, they will instantly have reason to question the strength of the fit. Most likely, they will dismiss that candidate and move on to the next.

I've heard voicemail greetings with loud music playing in the background, cars honking, kids playing, dogs barking—you name it. Again, these are distractions that set the wrong tone and can only make a negative impression. You don't want to send the message that you are "too cool" to take a professional voicemail greeting seriously, or that work is not a priority.

Avoid funny voicemail greetings or anything unconventional. You may think your Game of Thrones-inspired voicemail recording is clever (and maybe it is), but for every person out there who likes it, there will be plenty of others who see it as a turnoff.

Why take an unnecessary gamble? It is so easy to record something simple and polished. Err on the side of classy and professional.

ONE LAST LOOK

Before you hit "submit" on each application, review all

of your documents and online profiles one last time. By this point in the book, you understand the main themes we've covered so far: (a) focus on relevance, (b) be consistent, and (c) consider your image from the perspective of the professionals who will be evaluating it. Send everything off only after you feel confident about the following questions:

As you assess your application, ask yourself:

- Are your resume and supporting documents clean, concise, and easy to read?
- Is your content relevant and targeted specifically to the position?
- Have you eliminated extraneous fluff?
- Does your current title match the position you are applying for? Does your objective match as well?
- Does your current location match the city of the employer (or, if not, have you left your current location ambiguous)?
- Have you omitted anything important?
- Are your voicemail greeting and social media accounts "hiring manager ready?"
- If you were hiring for this position, would you select this applicant to move forward to the interview stage? Is it logical that they applied?

Pretend you're showing your resume to someone who

has no experience in hiring. Would they be able to clearly see that the application matches the opportunity? The connection should be that obvious.

When the i's are dotted and the t's are crossed, do one final gut check. Once you know you've done all the diligence you can, send the application. Now grab your yoga mat or a celebratory glass of wine (however you unwind!). You've earned a break from all this thinking and strategy. But once you're refreshed and rebalanced, there is much more to do. We still have a lot to cover, starting with a behind-the-scenes look at what happens next.

KEY POINTS IN THIS CHAPTER

Conveying relevance is key. Anyone who picks up your application should clearly see that your experience matches the requirements of the open position.

Provide enough content to impress, without overdoing it or padding with fluff. Hiring managers are looking for a reason to weed you out, so don't give it to them.

Be thoughtful about the content of your LinkedIn profile if you want to be found and pursued by recruiters.

Be cognizant of the image that you project at all times. Written content, phone interactions, photos, and social media profiles will all be scrutinized by employers, and they must be in alignment with the job you want.

Chapter Three

WHAT HAPPENS NEXT? A GLIMPSE INSIDE THE "BLACK HOLE"

You've submitted your application. Now what? Most people find this stage of the process the most frustrating because it's an unknown, and there is really nothing they can do until—and unless—they receive a response from the employer. Candidates often describe feeling as if their resume has gone into a black hole. They wish they knew what was going on behind the scenes; it's all just a big mystery.

I'm here to pull back the curtain and shed some light on what really happens during this elusive in-between stage. This chapter will lay out everything you should know between hitting the send button and actually showing up for an interview.

before we get into that, let's zoom out for a moment talk about the hiring landscape from 30,000 feet. ___ nittedly, I am a bit of a data geek. There are plenty of fascinating statistics out there on the economy, the job market, and hiring in general. So let's begin this chapter by examining some numbers. I think you'll find them eye opening.

KEY JOB SEEKING STATISTICS

As this book goes to print, here are some key job seeking stats:

- The average job opening attracts 250 resumes. (Glassdoor.com)
- Two percent of applicants are called in for an interview for a typical job opening. (Glassdoor.com)
- Fifteen percent of hires come from job boards. (Jobvite.com)
- Forty percent of hires come from employee referral programs. (Jobvite.com)
- Sixty-five percent of recruiters report that the biggest challenge in hiring is a shortage of talent. (Jobvite.com)
- Forty-eight percent of small businesses found too few or zero qualified applicants for job openings. (NFIB.com)

You might read these facts and figures and think, "Wow, it's really brutal out there." It seems that way on the surface, right? I encourage you to look a little deeper.

A very small percentage of applicants receive an interview, but a huge percentage of recruiters and employers agree that their biggest challenge is finding good people. They have also experienced receiving *zero* qualified candidates when running searches. Zero!

So yes, it's technically true that very few job seekers are getting traction. *But it's not because the fields are extremely competitive.* In fact, it's quite the opposite. Two percent of applicants are getting interviews because more than 90 percent of the applicant pool for each open position is unqualified, unpolished, or has somehow managed to turn off the hiring manager for some stupid reason, many of which we've already discussed in the previous chapter.

Think about that. The vast majority of the 98 percent are being ruled out because they deserve to be. They are applying for jobs they have no business pursuing, or they've been careless and unthoughtful with their applications. They are in over their heads or they have made a bad impression. Even the ones who might be decently qualified have blown their own chances and left the door wide open for other candidates who have done a better job at presenting themselves.

> The vast majority of the 98 percent are being ruled out because they deserve to be.

If you follow the strategies in this book, you'll be well on your way to consistently finding yourself in that 2 percent. So, let's continue forging ahead. In the previous chapters, we discussed how to prepare an effective application. Now let's take a deeper dive into what happens as it is being evaluated by an employer.

You are about to learn how an employer selects their elusive "short list;" the lucky few candidates who are selected to interview.

WHAT YOU ARE ABOUT TO READ MAY SHOCK YOU

Employers have an undisclosed mental checklist of items that weigh heavily in all of their hiring decisions. When I mentioned in the introduction that I can immediately predict with nearly 100 percent accuracy whether a candidate will get hired, it's because of my knowledge of this criteria. I have observed companies use it to make their hiring selections countless times throughout my career. Some employers are very aware that they use it, whereas others are oblivious to its impact on their decision making. Either way, the consistency in this checklist (regardless of industry, company, and position) is downright uncanny.

Are you ready for it? Here's the secret sauce:

- **Commute.** How far is the distance from the candidate's house to the employer's location? Yup, they will Google or Waze it—during rush hour.
- **Tenure.** Does the candidate have a demonstrated history of good tenure with a small number of companies? Or have they jumped around and had brief stints with various employers?
- **Relevance.** We've already talked this one to death. I know you get it. They're checking to see if the candidate's experience is a logical fit for the position and verifying that they actually have the background to do the job.
- **Title.** We've already addressed this as well. They look to verify that the candidate's current job title matches the open position (or is very close).
- **Industry.** Employers generally want to hire from their own industry whenever possible. If a construction firm is hiring an administrative assistant or an accounting professional, they will always try to pull a candidate out of another construction firm before considering someone from a manufacturing company, for example. Same industry background is always attractive, no matter what the position or level of seniority.
- **Preconceived Biases.** This one is sometimes a factor, sometimes not. And frankly, it is impossible to predict

or do much about. An employer might prefer to hire a woman for a particular position because the company's current executive board is all male and they want more diversity. Or perhaps a business owner wants someone over a certain age for a specific management role, because the existing employees in the department are on the more senior side, and there is a concern that hiring a younger manager might ruffle feathers. The possibilities are endless. You get the idea.

- **Special Qualifications.** Does the candidate have the non-negotiable special skills the employer is looking for? (Hint: these are almost always highlighted in the job description.) Again, these can be software proficiencies, languages, specific college degrees, and so on. Whatever the case may be for that particular opportunity.

- **Level of Polish and Professionalism.** Does the candidate present in a way that exudes class, both on paper and in their photos? Do they take their reputation seriously? Are they likely to represent the company well?

There you have it. The real criteria that employers use behind the scenes to establish their short list. Candidates' chances of being hired are literally made or broken based on these eight criteria every single day. They are what separate the 98 percent from the 2 percent.

You might be even more surprised to know these criteria don't just apply when there are huge numbers of applicants to consider. I see it happen all the time even in cases where there are a mere handful of resumes.

Earlier in my career, I remember one instance where I delivered two resumes to a client for a senior-level opening. Both were outstanding candidates and had been thoroughly vetted. I was so excited to present them. Almost immediately, I received the feedback on candidate #1: "Well, this person has an hour commute. That'll never work." And candidate #2? "Ugh, she's had two jobs in the past five years. We hire for the long term here, so we can't risk bringing in a job hopper." And then the dreaded, "Who else do you have?" Boom. Just like that, all my hard work was down the drain, and I was back to the drawing board.

It's important to note that I'm not saying these criteria necessarily *should* be used in the hiring process. In fact, there are times when I feel these criteria lead employers away from the right candidates. I err on the side of giving people a chance, within reason, and tend to see the gray in life. To this day, I still believe that my client passed over two phenomenal people, either of whom could have been a good fit in that job. It was disappointing, and in those cases I wish that the employer could have overlooked the commute and the tenure issues and seen the bigger picture. Oh, well.

Remember, this book is not about what I think, it's about what I *know*. It's the truth about how hiring decisions are actually made in the real world, regardless of whatever my, your, or anyone else's personal opinions on those tactics, strategies, and logic might be. As you read on, you'll begin to see things more and more from the employer's perspective and understand why this practically universal hiring criteria exists in the first place.

WHAT ELSE ARE THEY LOOKING AT?

If your application survives the first pass-through of those initial eight criteria, it may or may not be enough to land you an interview. That will largely depend on how many other candidates are in the same boat. If the company is hoping to interview five people for the position and five passed the initial litmus test, then all five are going to get a phone call. On the other hand, if the hiring manager only wants to interview the top three people, they have a bit more narrowing down to do. There are a few additional aspects they are likely to look at next in order to accomplish this.

- **Social Media.** This is where the social media exploration that we talked about in Chapter 2 could come in. You can bet at the very least that your LinkedIn profile will be reviewed, and probably your other social media accounts as well. Again, the employer is looking to see the face (literally) that goes with the name, and a quick first impression of how you present yourself to the world. Employers generally do a first pass of social media in cases where they are on the fence about someone. "Hmm, I'm not sure about this resume. Let me look the person up online and see what I can find." At this stage, they may see things like community involvement, charity work, industry group participation, or articles you've written, all of which are likely to make a positive impression. Pets are generally a home run, too, believe it or not, so don't hold back posting those photos of your four-legged friends. Basically, the employer is just looking to verify that you are a well-rounded, normal, decent human being who would make a respectable addition to their team.

- **Current Employer Research.** In some cases, the hiring firm may never have heard of your current employer, nor are they familiar with what the company does. If that's the case, they may dig deeper online. It's often as simple as going to the company website. The hiring manager is looking to confirm relevance here. They are hoping to learn that your current employer is similar enough in size, structure, and type of work that you'd have an easy transition into the new company. If you are applying for a property manager position overseeing commercial buildings, but then the HR person figures out that your current employer only has residential buildings in their portfolio, it could rule you out.

- **Stealth Reference Checks.** This is a big one that surprises a lot of people. It is common for a hiring manager to realize that they have a mutual connection with a particular applicant, and then reach out to that third party for an informal reference. It is usually a former boss, colleague, or industry connection of the candidate's whom the hiring manager knows personally. Either way, they will not hesitate to pick up the phone and say, "Hey, so-and-so just applied for a position over here, what can you tell me? What do you know about her?" You may never even know that the conversation took place, because you never listed the person as a formal reference. Remember, the world is small.

A METHOD TO THE MADNESS

It is important to understand that these hiring criteria are not random and do not exist for no reason. While they may seem odd and even unfair, employers do have their reasons for factoring them heavily in their hiring decisions.

We touched on flight risk earlier, but it is a concept that needs to be emphasized. When hiring, an employer's goal is more complex than just to determine the most qualified person for the job. Their aim is to identify the candidate most likely to do the job well *who will also stay with the company long term.*

> An employer's goal is more complex than just to determine the most qualified person for the job. Their aim is to identify the candidate most likely to do the job well *who will also stay with the company long term.*

Because employee turnover is so disruptive and expensive, it is always in a company's best interest to hire employees who stick with them. They literally can't afford flight risks, and they try to avoid them at all costs. Today more than ever, employers are hyper focused on predicting who will stay with them long term. Accurate predictions save companies tremendous amounts of money and man-hours each year.

Now go back to that list of hiring criteria and look again. When you originally read it, you probably thought, "Why on earth would the length of my commute be something that an employer would even think about?!" But considering it now through the lens of concern about flight risk, it starts to make a lot more sense. Commuting can be draining. Long commutes are not ideal. I can't think of ever hearing someone say, "I love sitting in traffic for multiple hours every day!"

Bottom line: that hiring manager is calculating your

commute out of concern that if it's too arduous, you'll get tired of it after a year or two and leave the company for another job closer to home. Particularly in big cities, if an employer has a choice between a candidate from the suburbs with a long drive to work versus someone with a downtown apartment who can walk to the office, it's obvious which scenario is preferable.

Same thing goes for lack of tenure. If you've moved around a bunch of times, a potential employer might worry that you are fickle, get bored easily, or don't know what you want. They worry, "If this person hasn't stayed committed to his previous employers for any length of time, what's to say he'll be committed to us?" Long commute and past job hopping are very real predictors of employee turnover. They are examples of gambles that employers won't take, at least not whenever they can avoid it.

Companies are also trying to avoid hiring people who are just a bad fit. Even worse than a flight risk is a toxic, underperforming, or disgruntled employee. Letting a bad match through the door can drag down an entire team, and even poison a company's culture under extreme circumstances. One bad apple can spread negativity like a cancer, which creates a whole other set of problems— not the least of which could be a mass exodus. Hello, employee turnover!

The point is, hiring is about so much more than filling an opening or putting a capable body in a seat. Hopefully by now you're starting to see how complex these decisions are, and why. The stakes are high for these companies. They need to get it right. At the end of the day, while their methods may seem questionable, they are just looking out for their own best interest. It's hard to fault anybody for that.

THE WAITING GAME

What do you do while the employer is working their way through the process of selecting their short list? Nothing. I know that's probably not what you want to hear, but it's the best strategy.

Back to the dating analogy: if someone is interested in you, *you will know*. Chasing an opportunity too hard is pointless, and counter-productive. It's best to make your interest known, and then observe what the other party does with that information. In a hiring scenario, you've already done what you can do by prepping your application properly and following any directions they have given you up to this point. You are in front of the hiring team, and they know that you are interested. Trust me: If they like you, they will call you. And if they feel you are the best fit, they will pick you. Plain and simple.

Nothing is more annoying to a hiring manager than

when a candidate calls at this stage "to follow up." I know, I know, you want to reach out to make sure that they received your application, see if there is anything else they need from you, and ask about next steps in the process. Please, just don't. Candidates who do this, especially this early in the process, are very quickly regarded as irritants. Not only will your follow-up not move the process along any further or faster, you'll run the risk of turning off the very people whose approval you are seeking. Just sit tight.

WHAT'S TAKING SO LONG?

Why do hiring processes take so long? There are many reasons. Sometimes companies just have a massive number of candidates and need ample time to get through them effectively. Maybe they want to leave the job posted online for a set period of time (say, a month) before even looking at the applications, to farm as many candidates as possible before the evaluation stage begins.

It is also very common for a job to be posted, but then put on the back burner—or off the radar completely. For example, a company might post a payroll associate position, but then a few days later their payroll manager quits. The manager role is a higher priority due to the level of seniority, and the fact that it will be tougher to fill. Suddenly it's all hands on deck and the entire HR team is scrambling to fill the manager position. The associate position is no longer a priority, and the HR team may not dig into that stack of resumes for weeks or even months.

Or a company may post a position, but then decide to fill it internally. They promote someone from within or they hire a referral from a current employee. Again, you could be the strongest candidate in the applicant pool, but you'll never get a phone call because HR didn't even look at the resumes.

The moral of the story is that there are many reasons why the hiring process takes a long time, and many reasons why you may not be contacted. Those reasons might have nothing to do with the candidate pool itself, and everything to do with some internal circumstance that you'll never know about. The delay could simply be because the manager is on vacation or maternity leave. You get the point. All the more reason not to chase down HR for status updates. They don't have time to be fielding those phone calls when they have other, higher-priority issues on their plate.

Also remember that silence is not necessarily a bad thing. Don't be surprised if you apply, hear nothing, and give up—only to wind up getting a call from the employer months down the road. This happens all the time! Maybe the dust has settled, and the position has become a priority again. Maybe their internal referral didn't work out. There are so many reasons why a search can be put on hold, and then resurrected later on. Always be prepared that the invitation to interview could come along when you least expect it.

It's easy to take this type of rejection personally, as if not getting called to interview is somehow a judgment of your self-worth. Always remind yourself that it's not. It really isn't. There is so much more going on behind the scenes, always. Let the company do what it needs to do and continue forging ahead with your search until someone shows an active interest in you. It will happen.

CONGRATULATIONS, YOU'VE MADE THE SHORT LIST

It's a wonderful feeling to get that call or email from an employer in response to your application. This is the first real sign that a company has an interest in potentially hiring you. It is a huge moment! It took a lot of effort to get to this point, so it's critical to keep the positive momentum flowing.

Let's talk a bit now about response times, because they are critical. I hear people say all the time, "Oh, I got a call this morning from such-and-such company, but I'm going to wait a couple of days before calling back. It'll give them the impression that I am in high dema: then they'll want me more."

It literally makes me cringe just writing that sentence! This mentality of "playing hard to get" absolutely kills me. Operating this way is honestly one of the dumbest things a job seeker can do. Delaying a response won't signal that you're in high demand. Instead, it will send a message that you're blasé, unmotivated, or just simply disinterested in the opportunity. Bad, bad, bad.

If you miss the call, return it promptly. If they email you, reply right away. Let's get real, we are all glued to our phones every day, and employers know that. There is no excuse for a long delay. To make the best impression, you should respond within a couple of hours, and preferably quicker than that.

Let's say the employer has selected a short list of five people, including you. The first four answer on the first ring or call back immediately, whereas you miss the call and take all day before responding. Imagine how that looks in the eyes of the hiring manager. He's now gotten the impression that he has a pool of four very interested candidates, and a fifth who could take it or leave it.

If you come across less motivated, I promise it will be noted and remembered. It won't necessarily ruin your chances completely, but why leave a poor taste when it's so easy to make a good impression? Response time will speak to your level of enthusiasm, as well as your communication skills.

Speaking of enthusiasm, employers like it. A lot. You never want to be over the top (remember what we discussed earlier about desperation), but conveying a genuine, believable enthusiasm is always a good thing. When you connect with the employer via phone or email, tell them sincerely that you're excited about the opportunity. They want to hire someone who wants to be a part of their team. Conveying that you want to work for a particular company is an often-overlooked component of winning them over.

Now, what do you do if the call comes through at an inopportune time? Perhaps you're in a meeting, or your boss is within earshot. Yikes! It's totally fine to answer and say, "I'm so happy you called. Can we schedule a time to talk later today?" Or better yet, "Can you hold for one moment? I just need to step into a more private area of the office." Those are your best options, both of which are palatable to any hiring manager.

Alternatively, if you try to take the call in a setting where you really can't speak freely, you won't convey the proper tone or energy. It will sound awkward and won't make a good impression. The hiring manager will wonder, "Did I catch this person at a bad time, or do they just have a terrible phone presence?" Rather than force your way through it, it's always better to ask to speak a little later or step elsewhere to take the call.

I think you will find that HR professionals are sympathetic to these situations. They understand not wanting to tip off your boss or one of your coworkers that you're actively looking for a new position. Just be polite and professional, while conveying enthusiasm and it'll be no trouble at all.

BE PREPARED

Presuming that you've just been called for the purpose of scheduling an interview, be sure to get the information you need to go in fully prepared and feeling confident. After you've confirmed the date, time, and location, here are some good (and totally appropriate) questions to ask for further clarity before you end that first call:

- How long should I plan to be there?
- With whom will I be meeting? Get names and titles.
- Is there anything I should bring to the interview?
- Is there anything in particular I should prepare?

Having this information ahead of time will enable you to do your homework on the people you'll be meeting with, which is a big deal. The better you know your audience, the better your ability to connect with them during the interview. Depending on your industry, it might also be appropriate to bring along some of your work product, like a design portfolio or writing samples. Your initiative in asking these questions makes a good impression and allows you to prepare thoroughly for the interview.

A candidate who is thoughtful enough to ask good questions demonstrates that they take the process seriously, are organized, and want to succeed in the hiring process. The HR person might say it's not necessary to bring work product, but I generally recommend bringing it anyway, if that's logical based on the role. In the event that HR mistakenly gave you the wrong information, you don't want to be asked for your portfolio during an interview only to say, "Well, so-and-so told me not to bring it." Embarrassing.

Also, just having it with you does not mean that you have to share it. Bring it along discretely and have it ready just in case someone asks. You may also want to show it regardless of whether you're asked, if you feel the interview is going really well and the timing feels appropriate. Exercise common sense. Having something of value to show demonstrates that you're proud of what you do, and it will give the hiring team a whole new level of insight into your capabilities. Even if you never do get to show it, there's no harm in having it with you.

If you're not sure of the perfect moment to bri'
your samples, here's a suggestion. As the conversฺ.
is winding down, say, "By the way, I brought a copy of my
portfolio. May I leave it with you, so you can take a look
after I leave?" This technique works because you're not
forcing them to take the time to review it in that moment,
but you are giving them the option to check out your work
at their convenience. It also opens the door for them to
respond by saying, "Oh, great! We'd love to see it. Why
don't you walk us through the materials before you go?"
We'll go much deeper into interview strategies in Chapter 4.

BEWARE OF THE IMPROMPTU SCREEN

Be aware that the first call might be a phone screen (that's
hiring industry jargon for "phone interview") in disguise.
Some companies ask a few questions of the candidate
right away on that first phone call, to get a better sense
of the person and feel out whether to invite them in for
a formal interview.

Needless to say, it's *really* important that you respond to
any questions thoughtfully and put your best foot forward. Employers hiring for positions that require a lot of
time spent on the phone are much more prone to conduct
on-the-spot preliminary phone interviews. Their goal is to
get an immediate sense of how a candidate comes across

over the phone, because that's an indicator of how they will represent the company if they are hired. If you owned a business, would you hire a low-energy, no personality, inarticulate person to do phone sales? Of course not. So, if you're trying to land a position that's remote or otherwise largely phone based, be prepared for an impromptu phone interview.

You'll know pretty much right off the bat if the call is going to be a screening interview. Either the person will say, "Thanks so much for applying. We really love your background. Let's set up a time for you to come in." Or, they'll say, "Thanks so much for applying. Can we chat for a few minutes? I'd like to ask you some follow-up questions."

When all else fails, maintain enthusiasm. If the caller closes the conversation without committing to set you up for a live interview, the best thing you can do is say, "I appreciate your time. I'm so excited about this opportunity. I really hope to hear back from you regarding next steps." Always end with great energy, because that leaves a positive and lasting impression.

KEY POINTS IN THIS CHAPTER

A mere 2 percent of applications are selected to interview for a typical job opening, but the majority of the 98 percent being ruled out deserve to be passed over. The field is not as competitive as the statistics make it seem.

Employers have an undisclosed set of criteria that they use in their hiring decisions. Being aware of it will help you position yourself for the jobs you want.

The goal of the hiring manager is not to identify the candidate most qualified for a particular job opening. Rather, it is to identify the candidate most likely to do the job well *and* stay long term.

Hiring processes can be lengthy for many reasons. Be patient.

When an employer contacts you, respond promptly and enthusiastically. First impressions matter.

Chapter Four

IT JUST GOT PERSONAL: HOW TO IMPRESS IN THE INTERVIEW STAGE

An invitation to the interview stage is exciting. You've worked hard to get here, and it's an ego boost to know that the hiring team likes you enough to want to meet you in person. But interviewing can also be intimidating. Now the pressure is on.

The first interview can make or break your chances of getting hired. The impression that you make in that first in-person meeting will either advance you to the final phase of the hiring process (basically into the top 1 percent), or formally end your chances of working for the company. The importance of this stage cannot be overstated.

Please, before you show up to the interview, be prepared. It amazes me how often people arrive with no real clue what they are interviewing for, or what the company is all about. If you do this, regardless of your reasoning or excuses, you are setting yourself up for failure. Hiring managers will advance candidates who take the process seriously. They have very little, if any, patience for anything less. You've made it this far; don't waste your time—or anyone else's—by showing up and winging it.

While the early stages of the application process are about survival and avoiding being weeded out, the interview stage signals an important shift. Now it's about making an interpersonal connection and giving the interviewers reason to *like* you. You're no longer a collection of informational bullet points on a piece of paper. You're now a human being, who will suddenly be dealing with other human beings.

Likeability and memorability take center stage.

> While the early stages of the application process are about survival and avoiding being weeded out, the interview stage signals an important shift. Now it's about making an interpersonal connection and giving the interviewers reason to *like* you.

Your goal is to leave the interviewers thinking, "Wow, I really liked that person. I could see them working here.

I'm looking forward to seeing them again and introducing them to my colleagues." This should be your driving focus. And if you can accomplish it, you're a shoe-in to move forward from there.

So how do you do that? This chapter will lay out the strategy, and the insights necessary to kill it in the interview.

THE X-FACTOR

At this stage, you must assume that all of the interviewees are qualified for the job, at least on paper. Otherwise they wouldn't have been invited to interview. Given that the playing field is relatively equal in that sense, the hiring team is now thinking, "Whom do we want to work with every day? Whom can we envision fitting in here?" Personality takes a prominent role because now you are being seen and evaluated as someone who could potentially be showing up to work side by side with these people every day.

Have you ever met someone randomly, and instantly gotten the sense that there is just something special about them? You can't really put your finger on it, but they are intriguing and exude genuine likeability. They make you want to be around them. My recruiting team calls that the "x-factor." We can't always define it, but we instantly know it when we see it. And when we come across a job seeker who has "it," our client hires them.

ry. Single. Time. Even when that person is technically qualified than the others interviewing.

People find it surprising that interpersonal connection and likeability often take precedence over hard qualifications, but it's not totally illogical. Think about it this way: There are generally multiple qualified candidates for any given job opening. If anyone on the short list can technically do the job, the relative tie has to be broken somehow.

Put yourself in the shoes of someone hiring for their own department. You're debating between three people, all of whom are qualified. Two have questionable personalities and cause you to watch the clock until the interview is over. The third one walks through the door practically sparkling—he exudes enthusiasm, and you enjoy your conversation with him. When it comes time to make a hiring decision, which one would you be inclined to pick?

It's human nature to gravitate toward someone you would look forward to seeing every day, versus someone who is going to annoy you. It is also common for employers to choose a phenomenally likeable, less-qualified candidate over someone with a perfect background who is not engaging in the interview. There are plenty of qualified people out there if you look hard enough, but those who have the x-factor are rare (and valuable) gems.

This is especially true in smaller companies. The smaller the total number of employees in an organization, the more closely everyone works together, and the more crucial it is that everyone vibe well. A single person in a start-up environment could be 10 percent (or more) of the entire company. In a 500-person firm, the group can much more easily withstand one bad fit without destroying morale. But that's not the case if there are only a handful of employees in total.

One of my small-to-mid-size clients focuses almost exclusively on personality during their interview process. Frankly, it used to drive my team crazy from the recruiter's perspective, because very little value was placed on candidates' resumes. We adapted, however, and quickly got very good at delivering what this client wanted. Once we figured out the personality prototype, it was easy to screen for. If a candidate was extremely outgoing, fun, had bubbly energy over the phone, and was the type of person who could hold a conversation with anyone, they were in. It was truly that simple.

Employers tend to be of the mentality that skills can be taught, but personality is what it is. I do agree there is a lot of truth to this. Hiring managers often opt to hire a slightly underqualified person and invest in training to get them up to speed. They would prefer to hire for personality and help that person grow into the role, as opposed to taking a gamble in an area that they know they won't be able to change.

Every company is different, and the particulars may vary. But the point remains: no matter where you are interviewing, likeability matters.

REVIEW THE ORIGINAL JOB POSTING

By the time you get the call inviting you to interview, it may be months since you originally applied. And if you have been actively job seeking throughout that time period, you've probably sent out a fair number of applications. The odds of you remembering all the ins and outs of the original job posting to which you applied are slim to none. Now is the perfect time to refer back and study the relevant job descriptions before each interview. You'll want to be 100 percent clear about what the position entails and what points the employer took the time to emphasize. These are clues as to what will be discussed in person, and what you'll want to be prepared to talk about.

Just as you took the time to draw parallels between your qualifications and the job requirements when you prepared your resume, you'll want to do the same thing in your interview. This in-person exchange is your opportunity to drive home how and why you and this company are a good match. Anywhere you can naturally weave these points into the conversation, you must clearly articu

how your experience is relevant to the job at hand.

YOU MUST HIDE DESPERATION
IN AN INTERVIEW

Desperation is a major turnoff. If an employer gets a whiff of it, they will feel sorry for you, but will move on and hire someone more confident. If you're feeling desperate, you must learn to mask it. Be poised and project a calm, thoughtful energy.

Have you ever met someone for the first time who is visibly nervous, and oddly overselling themselves to you? It's a big turnoff, isn't it? You probably thought, "Why is this person pushing so hard?" And, "Ugh, just calm down and be yourself!" It's the same concept in a hiring scenario. Desperation is irritating and unattractive, regardless of the circumstances.

Believe in your value and the talents you bring to the table. Wear something that looks good and makes you feel good. Anything you can do to ramp up your confidence before you step in that room will serve you well in your interviews.

You can say something like, "I'm currently between positions, but I want to make sure this is the right fit. It's very important to me that the next position I choose will be a long-term match." Now you're projecting selectivity rather than desperation—and that is a far more desirable trait. The employer will think, "If we make an offer to this candidate and she accepts it, she's saying yes because she really wants to be here—not because we're the first company to offer her a paycheck."

It is an enormous turnoff when a candidate shows up to interview and has vague (if any) recollection of the job description, what the company is looking for, and so on. Do not go into the in-person meeting thinking to yourself, "I forget, did they say they want someone detail oriented? Is prior management experience important? Which special skills are they looking for, again?" You can see how that conversation will get derailed very quickly. Without some insight into what the company is looking for in an ideal candidate, you can't convey why you are that person—and you've just lost.

If you're having trouble putting the pieces together or tracking down the original job posting prior to your interview, *ask*! My firm posts jobs to our company LinkedIn page, because we occasionally get quality applicants through that site. Sometimes when I call a candidate to follow up, they will say to me, "I'm sorry, do you mind reminding me which posting this is regarding? I'd just like to refer back and refresh myself." Personally, I am always happy to help orient the candidate, and never irritated by this question. At least I know that the person cares enough to get the information right and present their qualifications specific to the position at hand. This initiative and conscientiousness are admirable.

WHAT TO WEAR

Here's another point that frequently ruffles feathers, but really shouldn't: Your clothing, accessories, hair, make-up, and general personal appearance *do matter*, and will be judged when you interview. What you wear and how you present yourself in person is a significant aspect of the overall impression you convey to a potential employer. While this may sound intimidating, don't let it stress you out. The good news is that it's really not complicated to get it right. What *is* surprising is how frequently job seekers get it wrong.

Deciding what to wear is similar to preparing your resume, in the sense that you don't want to do anything that will get you eliminated. Now is not the time to be outrageous. Regardless of gender and personal style, classic and classy are always best. Dress appropriately for the position. You want to look good, but make it seem effortless at the same time.

Pretend that you are about to show up for your first day of work at the company. What would you wear to blend appropriately with the other employees?

TIPS FOR WOMEN

I'm not going to sugarcoat this: Women have it tough when it comes to interview attire. And not just because of the plethora of options available to them. For every woman out there who gets rejected because she is not "polished" or "pretty" enough, another is being turned down for being "too attractive" or "too trendy." Yes, I have seen candidates passed over for both reasons. Yes, it makes my stomach turn every time.

As women, we are basically damned if we do, damned if we don't when it comes to how we dress and groom ourselves, because people will always have a judgment about it. It's easy to dismiss that and say, "Okay, whatever," in our everyday lives, but when it comes to interviewing it's a lot harder to ignore. Now someone's judgment of us could actually cost us a *job*.

Yes, ladies, I know—it's awful. But it's the world we live in, and employers have their biases. All we can do is deal with it as best we can. To avoid the potential pitfalls and judgments that could stand in your way, take the following advice to heart and use it to your advantage. I have seen it work hundreds of times over, regardless of whether the interviewer is a man, a woman, young, old—whatever. It is foolproof.

Select a *dress* and keep it simple. I recommend navy, black, brown, hunter green, any dark neutral color you prefer. It should be at least knee length, with a basic silhouette that you feel comfortable in and that suits your body. There are tons of really beautiful, reasonably priced dresses out there that are simple, flattering, classic, and universally appealing. That's the look you're after. If you don't already own a dress like this, invest in one. It will be worth its weight in gold, trust me. If it's cold out or if you feel you'd be more comfortable adding another layer, pair the dress with a stylish suit jacket or cardigan of coordinating color.

If you're young or particularly fashionable and concerned that this look is too boring for your taste, spice it up with a sharp pair of heels, some tasteful jewelry, and a nice handbag. I know this may still seem conservative for some people, but it is always the best way to go, especially in a first interview. Sticking to classic, clean lines and colors, and avoiding anything too flashy helps you avoid the trap of, "She's too pretty," or "She's trying too hard." You may look absolutely stunning (you go, girl!), but strutting into an interview dressed like a fashion model is risky business. You're walking a dangerous line that may actually turn off your audience, particularly if the interviewer is older, or very conservative, or a less attractive woman. Your aim is to look your best, *without* going over the top or making fashion choices that will be distracting.

Just as being too physically attractive can work against you, I have seen women rejected for jobs because they were not polished enough. A couple of years ago, my firm was working with a phenomenal candidate who had made it successfully through four rounds of interviews. On paper, she was easily the top choice. She knew her stuff, was articulate, interviewed well, and did everything right. But she ultimately lost the job because of her appearance.

As you can imagine, it was a heartbreaker. How could this happen? Well, the position she was pursuing was client-facing, and the industry was luxury sales. As hard as she tried, this candidate just didn't have any real sense of style. She always looked plain, and borderline like she just didn't put much effort into her appearance (no manicured nails, no styled hair, and so on). "Plain" in this luxury industry translated to "frumpy" in the eyes of the hiring team and the owner.

At the end of the day, they did not feel that the candidate was polished enough to represent the company on the level necessary. They worried that their female clients in particular would not take her seriously. I will never forget the client telling me, "Jane can do this job with her eyes closed, but I just can't put her in front of my customers."

Again, ladies, I know—this is touchy stuff, and it's hard to hear stories like this without them hitting nerves. No woman wants to be judged on her appearance, and tone down or vamp up her look to please another person. Kind of like no woman wants to admit that she does the judging, out of jealousy or insecurity or whatever the case may be. But we all know it happens every single day. Male or female, you've seen and heard the cattiness and judgment in public and everyday life. It's no different in the workplace.

I also invite you to consider this perspective: You are not editing your look for the benefit of the employer; *you are editing your look for the benefit of you.* It's not about changing who you are, it's about putting your best foot forward. You're playing the game and taking control.

Many women have a perception that the prettiest person is most likely to get the job, but I'm here to tell you that that's only true about 50 percent of the time. Honestly, for every single employer I've heard say, "We will only hire good-looking people," I know another who refuses to hire attractive people out of fear that they will potentially be a "distraction in the workplace." The latter is quite common, particularly in male-dominated industries where HR is paranoid about inviting sexual harassment suits.

So regardless of where you perceive yourself to be on the scale of "attractiveness" or trendiness, my point is that it really doesn't matter. Biases abound, but they are so random and unpredictable that it's pointless to worry about them. Take my advice about the universal home run interview outfit, walk through the door well groomed, and you'll be positioned to make a positive, universally palatable impression.

> Biases abound, but they are so random and unpredictable that it's pointless to worry about them.

The only caveat I will add is that you need to know your industry and tweak your attire accordingly. If you are interviewing for a job at Vogue, for example, that's a unique environment where (I assume) exceptional personal style is likely to be a component of what will get you hired. By all means, if you work in fashion or some other industry where you know you can and should dial it up, show 'em what you've got.

What about interviewing in self-proclaimed "business casual" environments? My advice remains the same—stick with the neutral power dress. A simple, dark dress has incredible versatility. This outfit can hold its own in a room where everyone is dressy, but it's also simple enough that it won't seem over the top if everyone else is wearing nice jeans or slacks. You can blend in pretty much anywhere with this choice. Plus, when it comes to business casual it's always better to be slightly over dressed than under dressed, so don't fall into the trap of dressing down.

TIPS FOR MEN

Men have it far less complicated. Guys, your interview attire should align with the culture of the company and look appropriate for the position itself. If you give some simple thought to both of these aspects before you put on your outfit, you'll look perfectly appropriate.

In corporate environments, a classic suit and tie is the way to go. You can't go wrong, and it's essentially a guarantee that you will blend in with current employees. In business casual environments, skip the jacket and tie and opt for dress pants with a nice button-down shirt or a sweater. Again, it's damn near impossible for men to make a bad impression or be rejected over personal presentation. The only way they can screw up is by looking sloppy or totally inappropriate (e.g., disheveled clothing or grooming).

That said, men, you should always make an effort to dress for the job to which you are applying. I once had a client who was interviewing IT candidates. This was a large company with a very buttoned-up, conservative office culture, but their IT people had a reputation for being slightly less dressy than everyone else due to the nature of their work. They were constantly running between job sites, and setting up remote offices on construction sites, so they needed to be comfortable and agile.

When the interviews began, most candidates showed up

looking sharp, but relatively casual (nice pants, shirts, and sweaters). Then one guy came dressed in a full suit. Not that there's anything wrong with that, but he just seemed uncomfortable and out of place next to the others. He didn't look the part. My client just laughed it off as a little bit comical, and it was never discussed again—no big deal. But I always wondered how much that visual impression impacted their final decision, however subconsciously. (The guy in the suit didn't get the job).

Guys, you have it pretty easy (lucky you)! Dress like you already work for the company you're applying to, in the role that you are interviewing for. Comb your hair, brush your teeth, dry clean your shirt, wear nice shoes. It's not much more complicated than that. Put in a little thought and effort, and you will be just fine.

THE IMPORTANCE OF GOOD QUESTIONS

I have one particular client who flat out will not hire any candidate who does not ask questions in the interview, or who says something like, "Oh, you already answered all of my questions. I'm all set!" It's his biggest pet peeve, and many employers feel the same. Their logic is that if someone isn't interested enough to probe deeper or invested enough to think on their feet and come up with some original questions, they don't really want the job.

It's common knowledge that showing up to the intervie with good questions prepared is important. Doing so si nals initiative, sincere interest, and thoughtfulness. But many candidates struggle with what to ask.

Do not overcomplicate this. Be sincere. Rather than trying to think up questions for the sake of having a list, *think about what you actually want to know*. You are about to interview with a company that could potentially be your next employer. Naturally, you should have lots of questions!

Here's a good trick. Go back to the self-reflection work that you did back in Chapter 1. Remember those non-negotiables? Refer back and use them now to craft your questions for the interviewer. Did you have a rough relationship with your past manager because of a particular personality trait? I'd be asking some probing questions about your potential new manager, for sure.

The whole point of asking questions is to gain insight into the company and the open position. You are trying to determine whether or not it's a place you want to work, and a job you want to do, if an offer is made. Don't try to impress the hiring manager by thinking of smart questions. Think of genuine questions, and you'll impress the hiring manager automatically.

Don't try to impress the hiring manager by thinking of smart questions. Think of genuine questions, and you'll impress the hiring manager automatically.

If you are still struggling with this, here are a few good places to start:

- **The Position:** Get to the root of what the company is looking for in their ideal employee. What is the most important quality they are seeking? What specific skill or skills are most critical to success in the role? Was there someone in the position previously? If so, what happened and why are they no longer there? If the previous person was let go, why? This question alone can provide tremendous insight. What requirements in the job description are critical, versus which ones can they live without? You get the idea. Understanding how the employer sees the position—and their ideal candidate—will enable you to do a gut check, and really determine the strength of the fit.

- **The Culture:** This area is as important to explore as the role itself. There is a lot of ground to cover when exploring organizational culture. What is it like to work for the company day to day? Who is their "typical" employee? What are the organization's values, and how do those trickle down (or not) into the experience of working for the company? What types of challenges do new hires tend to experience? What personality traits are common among employees in the company? How would current employees describe the culture? What is the tenure rate? (Translation: are employees happy here?) Do not neglect this area of questioning. It may sound like "soft stuff," but the environment you're working in has the potential to have a real impact on your psyche and your work life. Again, refer back to your list of non-negotiables. Get to the bottom of whether or not this company sounds like a match for you.

· **The Company and the Leadership:** Asking more factual questions about the company and its leadership team can also provide helpful insight. How long has the organization been around? Are they growing? Has the growth been a consistent trajectory, or have there been bumps in the road, like layoffs? How long have the executives been involved? What are the C-suite leaders like, and how involved are they at all levels? What are they envisioning for the future? What are some of the strategic initiatives they are working on right now? These types of questions can spark some interesting dialogue and provide deeper insight into whether you can see yourself in the organization for years down the road.

Here's another thought: Remember when we talked about negative company reviews, and how those might be concerning? If you're interviewing with a company that has some bad press out there, that might be a great topic to inquire about in your interview. Be polite, but upfront and say something like, "I saw a couple of negative reviews online that seemed to indicate X. Can you speak to this?" It's a fair question. You might even find that the person you're speaking with is relieved to have the opportunity to tell their side of the story. Sometimes employers are not even aware that negative things are being said about them, and they appreciate that fact being brought to light graciously. It's a bold move on your part, but usually a gamble worth taking.

NEVER "GO NEGATIVE"

At some point during every interview, you are bound to be asked, "Why are you looking for a new opportunity?" Or, "Why did you leave your previous jobs?" This question opens the door for you to unload about all the things you're unhappy about in your current position, or your past positions, and paint those employers in a generally negative light. Do not fall into this trap.

Never, ever say anything negative about a past or current employer. If you do, it's an instant kiss of death. Over the years I have had many of my own candidates turned down for jobs because they went negative in an interview. Yes, I coached them beforehand not to do this. No, they did not listen. And yes, they regretted it after the fact.

I think people sometimes say negative things without even realizing that they are doing it. Be overly cautious about this, always. If a thought comes to mind and you even question whether it might be perceived as negative, better to hold back and not say it.

Why does going negative on past employers bother future employers so much? For a couple of reasons. The most logical reaction is, "Wow, if this person is saying awful things about the last couple of places he worked, what will happen if he comes here and leaves? Will he publicly bash our company, too?" They may also wonder, "Is this person just negative in general?" We all know there are people in this world who are chronic complainers who bring turmoil and drama on themselves. No sane, productive person wants to surround themselves with negative people, let alone hire them. A toxic, disgruntled employee is a liability to any business. By speaking negatively, you've just raised the flag that you might be one of them.

Smart hiring managers also know that every story has two sides, and the truth is generally multifaceted. When they hear a candidate say something negative, it compels them to want to find out what really happened. They won't hesitate to find a reference who can speak to the other side. It's human nature to think, "Hmm, that story sounds pretty terrible, but what would your old coworkers say about you and how you contributed to the conflict?"

Again, the dating analogy applies. If you're on a date with someone who tells you that all of their exes were completely insane, wouldn't that immediately raise a red flag in your mind? When any person has a string of bad experiences, *they* are the common denominator. Your antenna will go up, and you'll think to yourself, "There's got to be more to this story."

Always stay upbeat and positive in interviews. Obviously, it doesn't need to be all unicorns and rainbows, and you should be yourself. But you must project a positive general attitude. If you had a legitimately terrible experience with a past employer, avoid the subject as best you can or find a way to spin it into something positive (or at least neutral).

Another strategy is to make it about you and not them. Remember the example I mentioned earlier about the young woman who worked with all the extroverted coworkers? She could have gone into her interviews saying, "I'm really unhappy in my current situation. I hate it. Everyone is constantly socializing and it's exhausting to me. I feel peer pressure to be out drinking with them all the time. Even the owners act like they are still in college and I can't take it anymore." Alternatively, she could have spun it like this, "My current company has been really good to me and has taught me so much. I'm incredibly grateful for everything that I have learned there, but I feel it's time for me to move on. My skillset is more suited for long-term relationship building as opposed to quick-hit direct sales. I feel that I can be happier and more effective in a different environment that focuses more on quality over quantity." Huge difference, right?

WHAT IF THEY ASK ABOUT SALARY?

At some point during the interview process you're going to be asked, "Can you share your salary requirement?" Or some variation of the same. Don't let it catch you off guard. Compensation is a touchy and personal area for both candidates and employers alike. Give this matter careful thought before you interview and go in prepared to deliver an answer that feels right for you.

At the time of this writing, it is illegal in some states for a potential employer to ask a candidate, "What is your current salary?" or "How much are you making now?" That doesn't mean they don't still ask it all the time, so even if you're in one of the states where it's forbidden, don't be surprised if you find yourself on the receiving end of this invasive question. How you respond is really up to you. While you are never obligated to disclose your current salary, I do recommend keeping a couple of things in mind.

The reason employers ask this question is because they

don't want to waste their time on a candidate whose requirements are misaligned with what the company is comfortable paying. Let's say an employer has budgeted $50,000 for a position, and they absolutely cannot go above $55,000 out of fairness to current employees in the same department and their comparative pay grades.

During the interview process the hiring manager zeroes in on a great candidate, only to find out that she is already making $70,000 and wants a minimum of $75,000 in order to make a move. Not going to happen. It's a mismatch, and the employer would rather know that sooner than later. They'll want to move on to the next candidate, and limit the amount of time wasted.

I recommend getting really honest with yourself about your salary *expectation*, and then communicating that number when asked the salary question. If you're making $100,000 and you just won't leave your current employer unless you receive a significant bump in salary, tell the hiring manager that you "need to be in the $120,000 range." This allows for some flexibility, while also providing the ballpark figure needed to determine whether or not the numbers align.

On the other hand, if you are making $100,000, but are absolutely miserable at your job because you can't stand the company culture (or whatever), you might tell the hiring manager that you are "hoping for $100,000, but negotiable for the right opportunity." This communicates to the employer your desired salary, but also leaves wiggle room for them to offer you less if their budget is lower. The positive is that you'll be less likely to be ruled out over a salary mismatch, and it's a smart move if you truly are negotiable.

Sometimes quality of life is more important than the exact dollar figure. Only you can determine your own salary bookends, what you are willing to accept, and where it makes sense to gamble a little bit.

Focus on expectations rather than current earnings, and always be upfront. There is no point getting all the way to the end of the process and then having to reject an offer because you get lowballed. Better to err on the side of honesty and get it all out in the open. If you are the top candidate, everyone's cards will be on the table soon enough anyway. Why delay the inevitable?

One final note on this topic: When asked about salary, whatever you do, do not dodge the question. Employers hate this. By saying something like, "We can talk more about compensation later," or "I prefer not to talk about money," you are running the risk of seriously annoying the hiring team and being labeled as difficult, high maintenance, or disingenuous. No bueno. Keeping your number close to the vest won't do you any favors. Plus, again, evading the issue just leaves the door open for the employer to make you a low offer because they have no concept of your starting point. In this scenario, nobody wins. Just be honest.

ANOTHER WORD ABOUT COMPENSATION

Compensation is another piece of the hiring equation that candidates tend to take very personally, but shouldn't. Here's another little tidbit from an insider's perspective: employers budget for *positions*, rather than people. In other words, they have a dollar figure (or a rough range) in mind for every single position within the organization. Every role has its price tag, and there is generally minimal flexibility.

So, when a company tells you that you are "too expensive," or "out of salary range," it's not a reflection on you. The company is not saying that you, personally, are not worth the amount of money you're asking for. What they *are* saying is that they can't afford you, or that in their organization the value of that specific job is less than your own price tag.

It's not about you, it's about them. Salary is about the position, and the worth that the company has assigned to it. Which, by the way, is a determination that was made long before they even knew you existed as a candidate.

Some firms have *very* tightly defined salaries assigned to each position, literally to the dollar, which are completely and totally non-negotiable. Senior project managers make exactly $125,000, entry-level sales associates make exactly $42,000, whatever the case may be. The numbers are what they are, and they will not change regardless of a potential employee's individual qualifications.

Now, the more senior the level of position, the more flexibility there tends to be in pay negotiations. There is more room for negotiation in pay range for a COO, for example, than for an entry-level admin. Be aware of where you are on the seniority ladder and remember that pay ranges get broader as you climb higher.

A TWO-WAY CONVERSATION

The best interviews are the ones where both parties leave feeling as though they connected on a human level. It should be so much more than, "I'm getting asked questions, and I'm answering them." Your goal should always be a back and forth, natural dialogue. I know that this is easier for some people than others, and of course the ease will depend largely on the natural chemistry between you and the interviewer. But do your best, regardless, and know that a natural two-way conversation is what you are striving for.

Be engaging. Set the intention that you are showing up

to have a conversation, rather than answer a stranger's questions. Share personal anecdotes and stories as it feels appropriate. Look for common ground with the interviewer and point it out where you see it. Read their online bio or LinkedIn profile before you meet with them. Do you have a close friend or family member who attended their college? Do you share a personal hobby? Did you play the same sport? Do you share a passion for the same charitable cause? Highlighting commonalities can go a long way toward building a genuine connection with the interviewer.

When all else fails, smile.

WRAPPING UP THE INTERVIEW

Before you walk out the door, it is certainly acceptable to ask, "Assuming we do move forward from here, what would be the next step?" Generally, if the hiring manager has a strong interest in you at this point, they will say, "I would definitely like to move you on to round two, and you'll be speaking with so-and-so."

It is also fair to ask about timing. "What is your time frame for filling the position?" Or, "How far along are you with the first round of interviews?" The interviewer might say something like, "Well, we just got started, so we need a couple of weeks to work through the process."

Or, "We're winding down first interviews now and will be selecting the final two candidates by the end of this week." Regardless of their specific response, the answers will give you a reasonable idea of what to expect going forward.

Keep in mind that hiring processes really do not have standard time frames. It is hard for HR to predict exactly what will happen. I have seen some searches go on for months whereas others close in days. So much of the timeline is circumstantial, and can change on a dime, so take the answer you're given as a rough guideline and do not be surprised or overly concerned if it changes.

OVERQUALIFICATION

Being told that you're overqualified is one of the most dreaded and baffling pieces of feedback for any candidate to receive. Candidates apply knowing that they're totally capable of doing the job, and they wonder, "Why didn't I get picked? I'm more than qualified." Yes, exactly. You're overqualified.

That's a problem because the hiring manager worries that you won't be a long-term fit in the role. They think you're likely to leave for a job that will be more challenging and a better match for your level of experience. The last thing an employer wants to do is fill a position now, only to be back at it again in a few months. They want a long-term fit. They are trying to avoid turnover.

Employee turnover is incredibly expensive and disruptive to companies, and preventing it is a major objective of business owners, executives, and HR teams alike. Hiring decisions are so much more complicated than just "who can best do the job." Often even more than hard qualifications, employers are evaluating and selecting candidates based on who appears to be the best long-term play. Companies want employees who will be a great fit in their organization—not just at the time of hire but ideally for many years down the road. When screening candidates, hiring managers are always thinking, "Is this person likely to stay for a few years at least? Or are they going to see this job as a stepping stone to something else, and quit as soon as a better opportunity comes along?"

> When screening candidates, hiring managers are always thinking, "Is this person likely to stay for a few years at least? Or are they going to see this job as a stepping stone to something else, and quit as soon as a better opportunity comes along?"

If you're told that you are overqualified for a position, the employer believes they're doing you a favor by not picking you. Perhaps they are right. Take it as a blessing in disguise. Remember, a good long-term fit is also the best-case scenario for you. Trust the employer's judgment. Be grateful that they have helped you avoid a potentially unsatisfying experience (and a short stint on your resume that wouldn't be easy to explain). Better, more suitable opportunities are out there for you. Take the feedback as a compliment and move on to the next.

WILL THERE BE A SECOND DATE?

Time for another good old dating analogy (they work so well). Imagine yourself on your way home after a first date. You are probably spending the car ride digesting the experience, and you're likely to be feeling one of three ways: (1) you're on a high, elated, and can't wait to see the person again; (2) you are thinking, "Thank God that's over with," and have every intention of dismissing them if they text or call you asking for a second date; or (3) there isn't much rumination at all (you're already on to other thoughts) because the date just was not remarkable in any way. It wasn't horrible, but it didn't leave you excited. It was just blah, and forgettable.

When interviewing, there is only one kind of "date" you want to be. Your goal is to be the person who sends the interviewer home thinking, "That was a great conversation. I am intrigued by this person, and I'm looking forward to seeing where this goes." You need to be memorable—in a good way. If the hiring manager goes home after your interview feeling happy that it's over (worst-case scenario) or having already forgotten you because the conversation was so unremarkable (basically just as bad), your chances are shot.

It is important to note here that these impressions go both ways. Just as you are being judged and evaluated in an interview, you should be forming your own opinions about the employer. This company could potentially be your next workplace. It is just as important that you find the organization and its people likeable.

It is perfectly normal for candidates to walk out of an interview and think on their way home, "I really did not like the person I met with," or "I don't see myself fitting in at this company." If you're unsure of how you're feeling, here's a good litmus test: Close your eyes, drop into your gut, and imagine yourself getting the call inviting you back for a second interview. What is the *very first emotion* that you feel? Is it excitement? Happiness? A negative, sinking feeling? Total indifference? Something else? Now you have your answer.

If you're feeling down on an opportunity, best to pull yourself out of the running and move on. If you're feeling indifferent, I recommend sticking with the process a bit longer and obtaining more information before you make any decisions. But do get clear about what is hanging you up, so that you can delve deeper into those areas and get the answers you need in the next phase.

AFTER THE INTERVIEW

The period of time between the first interview and next steps can be tough for candidates. They are anxious to know "how they did," and what will happen next. Maybe they have their heart set on this job. Perhaps they are nervous about what's to come or frustrated that they're being held in limbo longer than anticipated.

Whatever the case may be, and as difficult as it is to be patient and wait, that really is what you need to do. Wait. Do not pester the hiring manager. You've already made it pretty far along in the process. They know who you are, and you are on the radar. The first interview is over. What happens next is in the hands of the employer. Your only job now is to sit tight.

Now, immediately following the interview, there is one concrete action that you can *and should* take. Always send a handwritten, personalized note thanking your interviewer. If you met with multiple people during the first interview, send each individual their own note.

The purpose of this exercise is simply to show gratitude for gratitude's sake, because it is the right thing to do.

You should ask for nothing in return. Do not request a response, and do not press the recipient for timelines or feedback. Simply thank them for their consideration and communicate your sincere, continued interest in the opportunity.

> Always send a handwritten, personalized note thanking your interviewer.

Candidates almost never send handwritten thank you notes anymore. Looking for a way to stand out? It's as simple as sending a handwritten card. I'm serious. Thoughtfully written, personalized thank you cards are a lost art. Taking the time to craft and send one always impresses hiring managers, because it conveys the message that you are considerate, respectful, professional, and taking this opportunity seriously. You care and are making the effort to further build a personal connection. That initiative goes a long way.

If you live in a different city and are worried about the lag time between when you send the card in the mail and when the person will receive it (you don't want them thinking for two or three days after the interview that you didn't thank them), I recommend sending a brief email on the day of the interview, followed by mailing a personal handwritten note. The interviewer will receive your email immediately, which prevents them from thinking, "This candidate didn't send a follow-up."

Then, when they least expect it, they will receive your handwritten card a couple of days later and think, "What a classy move." It's also a great strategy because it creates two touch points. First, the recipient will acknowledge the email as common courtesy. Second, they will appreciate the card and the effort you put into it. Now they've thought of you twice in a positive light since your interview. Whether you get the job or not, you have done the right thing.

Before you get writing and sending those cards, there is one huge word of warning which I strongly advise you to heed: *Never send a generic thank you note.* If you write a couple of vague, cliché sentences, the hiring manager is going to roll their eyes and think, "Ugh, this candidate is obviously sending the same damn note to every single company she is applying to." In an instant, your note can actually do you more harm than good.

If a thank you is not sincere or personalized, it loses its value. It will make you look lazy, and as if you didn't care enough to put some actual thought into what you were doing. It's a turnoff. Some employers are more sensitive to this than others, but I do have one client who has a habit of rejecting otherwise solid candidates over generic thank you notes. True story! His attitude is, "You sent me this totally impersonal note, which required practically zero effort and probably went out to twenty different companies. If I'm not special, neither are you." And boom, the candidate is out. It's an extreme example, but real people have lost out on real jobs with this company over this misstep. If thank you notes are such a hot button for this client, I am sure that there are other employers out there who feel the same way.

So how do you craft a note that will be well received? It's all about personalization. Make an impression by referencing specific items that were discussed in the interview. Play on a personal connection. Incorporate little points of interest to show that you tailored your note specifically to that company, and that opportunity. Explain why you feel *that* job and *that* company are the right fit for you. (It's that whole relevance thing again).

As far as the actual physical card is concerned, you'll need to determine what is most appropriate for your industry and the specific person you're sending it to. If I meet a male executive whose personality is very dry, I'm going to opt for a card that is neutral in color and conservative in style because it's a safe choice.

On the other hand, if I meet a female executive who has a big personality and we've learned that we share a love of animals, I'd hunt for a card that is girly and fun in style, perhaps with a dog or two on it. Play to the crowd, and when in doubt, go the traditional route. You might even consider getting your own custom stationary with a fancy monogram. I've seen candidates use these, and they are always a universally appealing, elegant choice.

KEY POINTS IN THIS CHAPTER

Likeability and personality take center stage in the interview phase.

Physical appearance matters and will be judged.

Be honest about your salary expectations, and keep in mind that companies have budgets allocated for each position.

Never go negative in an interview. Stay positive and classy.

Always send a thoughtful, personalized thank you note to your interviewer following your in-person meeting.

Chapter Five

SO CLOSE, BUT YET SO FAR: STAYING ON TRACK IN THE FINAL STAGES

The first interview is behind you. Your thank you notes have been sent. Now what?

You might be tempted to think that the process is winding down, and now you can sit back, relax, and see if you'll receive an offer. Rarely the case. Every company's hiring process is unique, but additional steps between the first interview and the offer phase are almost always to be expected. You're not done yet! In fact, you're about to enter potentially the most intense phase of the entire hiring process.

By now, the employer probably has the field narrowed down to two or three top candidates. These are the best of the best, any of whom are capable of doing the job, and all of whom managed to impress during the interview. If you've made it this far, you're in a good position. Your odds have gotten vastly better.

But now it's fiercely competitive, because all remaining candidates are strong and capable. The employer has a tough decision to make. Anyone still standing should prepare themselves for some very real scrutiny in the days or weeks to come.

If you really have your heart set on the job, you're probably feeling anxious by this point. Anxiety coupled with the unpredictability of what's to come can be a recipe for disaster, and even a candidacy derailing. Now you'll need to maintain positive momentum throughout these final stages until an offer is made.

In this chapter we'll explore some of the common challenges that candidates encounter in this phase between first interview and offer, and how best to overcome them.

FIRST THINGS FIRST: WHY CAN'T THE EMPLOYER JUST MAKE UP THEIR MIND?!

Sometimes hiring processes move rapidly through the initial review, weeding, and first interview stages, only to slow *way* down post-first-round interviews. Seems counter-intuitive, right? There are only a few candidates remaining by the end, so doesn't that mean a final selection should be easy at this point? Why can't they just pick A, B, or C?

The short answer is: it's complicated.

For the employer, now it's getting real. They are about to select an employee—someone who will essentially join their family, and whom they will invest in both financially and otherwise. It's a major commitment. As we've discussed already, the employer must get it right. The pressure is on, and this phase is when they start to really feel it. They have more homework to do before they extend an offer to one of the final candidates. They need to dig deeper to make the most informed decision possible.

Some companies complete the final steps in just a few days. Others take weeks or even months. It all depends on their process, the number of candidates, the number of steps remaining, and the comfort level of the hiring team when it comes time to pull the trigger.

ADDITIONAL INTERVIEWS AND SHADOWING

Almost always, there will be additional interviews. Sometimes these will entail meeting additional people the company. Maybe your first interview was with an HR manager and the second interview was with a department head or the person who could potentially be your direct supervisor if you get the job. There might be a second interview with the same person you met initially. Other possibilities include an interview with a group of people, or a series of shorter, private meetings with multiple decision makers scheduled back-to-back all in one day. Again, every company's process is different.

If you do get asked to interview with additional employees, go in as prepared as possible. Be sure to ask for the names and titles of anyone you'll be meeting and look them up online. Read their bios, review their LinkedIn, and so on. The information you find will help orient you and might also bring to light some common ground that you can touch upon when you meet the person.

You may also be asked to spend a day "shadowing" a current employee. I work with a few clients that incorporate this into their process. If the chance to shadow is offered to you, you should absolutely accept. A shadow day will give you an inside look at what life at the company is really like. Shadowing is great because not only does the company get to know you better, but you will get to know the company on a much deeper level. The knowledge gathering goes both ways.

You will walk away having seen the company and the
up close and probably even gotten to meet your poten
coworkers. Refer back to the self-assessment you did at
the beginning of this book; if you had something on your
list of non-negotiables like, "Need to be on a supportive
team with coworkers I enjoy," a shadow day will be particularly helpful to you. You'll get to spend hours with
the very people you'll potentially be working with, which
will help tremendously in determining if this is the right
opportunity for you. When the shadow day is over, you'll
come away with a strong sense of the culture and expectations that you could not possibly have gained through
interviews and conversations alone.

Another powerful aspect of shadowing is that it's an
opportunity to downshift from the mode of selling yourself. You'll be able to relate on a purely peer-to-peer level.
You may discuss aspects of the nitty-gritty (parking, work
schedules, the lunch room, interpersonal inside scoop,
etc.) that otherwise wouldn't be brought up in a formal
interview setting.

Good questions to ask include, "How do you like working
here?" "How long have you been here?" "What attracted
you to the company, and what is causing you to stay?"
"What are the people like?" "What do you dislike about
being here?" "What can you tell me about the boss?"
"Does the company promote from within?"

Take advantage of this opportunity to dig in and learn about whatever is truly important to you from the perspective of someone who is already living it. Most employees are pretty open and honest when asked by a candidate about their experience at a company. At the peer level, it makes no difference to them whether you accept the job or not. They have no reason not to give it to you straight.

TOP-LEVEL SIGN-OFF

Oftentimes, companies select their final candidate and then pass the "chosen one" up to the CEO or other top executive for a final blessing before the formal offer is made. This higher-up doesn't want, need, or have time to be involved in the minutiae of the hiring process, but they do want to be looped in and make sure they feel good about the choice before anything is finalized.

If you get called to meet the owner or CEO, that's an excellent position to be in. It's a pretty clear indication that you are the last person standing. They want you, and the final meeting should just be a rubber stamp. Most of the time, the CEO will approve, because everyone under them is vouching for you and saying, "This is our chosen candidate." It is very rare that an owner or CEO will challenge their team this late in the game. Although, I have seen it happen.

To avoid blowing it at this stage (talk about a heartbreaker), bring everything you've got to this final conversation. (Do not get cocky or lazy now!) Enter the meeting confident and fresh, as the same person you have been throughout the entire interview process up to this point. After all, whatever you have been doing has gotten you this far and earned you the buy-in of every other critical decision maker. Stay consistent. If you are feeling nervous, remind yourself that you've earned the spot you are in. You have people behind you, propping you up, because they have decided that you deserve to be there. That's a powerful confidence booster.

It is impossible to predict what the CEO will ask, or what the tone of the conversation will be. Some of the CEOs crank through these "interviews" in five minutes, just laying eyes on the candidate, exchanging a few pleasantries, and that's it. Others have favorite interview questions that they love to ask and might throw a couple of curveballs to see how the candidate responds. Either way, go with it and handle yourself as confidently as you can. Remember, even that CEO is rooting for you to do well, because the last thing they want to do is turn you down and start the search all over again.

WHAT IF THEY ASK ME TO TAKE A TEST?

Some employers incorporate different skill or personality assessments into their hiring process. They do this because the open position may require specific technical skills or behavioral traits. Subjecting candidates to various testing gives the employer another layer of information to consider and a more in-depth understanding of the remaining candidates. For example, it's one thing to state on your resume that you are an expert in Microsoft Excel, but will your test scores indicate the same? If Excel is a key component of the open job, the employer needs to know how concrete your skills really are.

Most of the time, the employer will send each candidate a link via email that will direct them to the appropriate place to complete the test online. Once the applicant does so, she may receive the results right away, or later in the process, or sometimes even not at all.

Usually, the company will quickly review the results, verify that they look solid, and stick them in a file along with your other application materials. In the event that an applicant's test scores are completely off base and raise a red flag, the candidate could be ruled out without further consideration. Generally, however, the reviewer will see the results as one more piece to the hiring puzzle, to be analyzed in conjunction with everything else.

Employers may also craft interview questions specific to you based on your results. Let's say you take a behavioral assessment and the results indicate that you have a tendency to be sensitive to constructive criticism. In the interview, you may get asked to describe some examples of negative feedback you have received from supervisors. The hiring manager is looking to see how you respond to that question, to further verify or debunk the assessment results. If you respond defensively, it will signify that the test tapped into something accurate. If the question does not faze you and you can have an open dialogue about it, the interviewer will likely determine that component of your results to be a fluke. Their goal is to fish out if the test results raised a legitimate red flag, or if they are nothing of concern.

If asked to take a test or assessment, do take it seriously. Also, do not try to "outsmart" personality assessments. It can backfire. Remember, you never know exactly what ideal results an employer is looking for. Your best bet is to simply answer the questions honestly. I know it can be intimidating to think that your responses to a few simple questions could make the difference between getting hired and getting rejected, but look at it this way: If your skillset or your personality isn't a match for particular role, it's not the right job for you anyway. Better to know upfront and be turned down, as opposed to being selected and getting in over your head and ending up miserable. These tests are used for a reason. They help employers ensure that they are making good decisions. And that's good news for you, too.

Now, I know most of us hate tests and the thought of taking them. I've seen candidates get offended when told that a test was required if they wanted to advance to the next stage of the hiring process. Just remember, it's not personal. It's not a reflection on you, or anything to get worked up about. You're in the same boat as every other candidate. Go with it.

Once you have received the link, take the test promptly. Even if you're nervous and want to put it off to prepare or study (which is impossible to do effectively anyway), procrastinating is a bad idea. The delay will signal to the employer that you're not motivated. They'll be more inclined to favor the candidates who act promptly. So, take a deep breath and just get it done. It's all good.

Sometimes when there are lots of hoops to jump through during the application process, it's by design. The company is trying to weed out who really wants the position, versus who just blindly applied for a hundred jobs to see what sticks. Whatever they stipulate, do it—that is, assuming you really want the job.

SPECIAL PROJECTS

A company may also ask you to complete a special project, for the purpose of affirming your capabilities in a specific area. This could include a case study, a live presentation, or something similar. Generally, the employer will provide you with a set of instructions and guidelines for the project, and you will be asked to submit or present it to the hiring team on or before a specific deadline.

If a special project is requested of you, again, it usually means you are one of the top two or three candidates still in play. The employer wants to see you in action. Take the task very seriously and put real thought into your project or presentation—even if it takes hours to complete. Yes, you are being asked to do work for free. But it's worth it, because the person whose final product is the most thoughtful and thorough will almost certainly get the offer.

REFERENCE CHECKS

It is practically guaranteed that if you've made it this far, you'll be asked for a list of references. This is another good sign that the employer is getting serious about you. Serious enough that they want to understand what you're all about, from people who know you firsthand—your former supervisors and colleagues.

LIST PREPARATION

Rather than including your references' names and numbers on your resume, I recommend creating a separate document. Keep it handy and ready to pass along when you are asked, rather than providing the information upfront. There are a couple of reasons why this is a better strategy.

First, it protects the privacy of your references. If I'm serving as a reference for someone, I wouldn't want my cell phone number or email address plastered all over job boards for everyone to see. Second, it enables you to keep track of which companies are actually conducting reference checks. If they ask you for the list, you'll know that they have a sincere enough interest in you that they're planning to make those calls.

Conversely, if you sent the reference information at the beginning of the process, the employer will have the ability to just call whenever, and you'll never know since they had no reason to prompt you for the information. Furnish your reference list separately, and only when asked.

Always create the reference list before you begin applying for jobs. It should be polished up and ready to go as soon as an employer asks for it. When you get the request, "Can you please provide a few professional references?" you'll want to send it quickly. The employer is ready to follow up, and they will not want to wait for days while you pull a list together.

WHOM TO SELECT?

The best references are people who have supervised you directly: your former bosses. Select people who know you well and have the authority to speak to what you can actually do. The purpose of reference checks is to gain an idea of what type of employee you will be, so you want to choose references who can paint that picture effectively.

Do not include former coworkers. Even if your associates say wonderful things about you, their opinions will not carry as much weight as those of a supervisor. In fact, it is considered a big fat red flag when a candidate provides a list of references that contains no direct supervisors. Immediately the hiring manager will wonder, "Why does this candidate not have any former bosses who will vouch for her?" That's a scary thought, right? In a case like this, HR may circle back to the candidate and ask specifically for names and numbers of direct supervisors. Or, they may take it upon themselves to call the HR departments of your previous employers and do some digging.

> It is a big fat red flag when a candidate provides a list of references that contains no direct supervisors.

If you got fired or had a personality clash with your boss, HR from your old company will have a record of it, and the truth will likely come out. To prevent these investigative calls from happening, include enough legitimate references from other places you've worked that the hiring manager will be satisfied and only need to call the names you provided.

You are never obligated or expected to include a reference from your current employer. It's rare for your current place of work to know that you are applying, except in special circumstances (maybe the firm is downsizing and you'll be laid off soon, so your current boss has offered to serve as a reference). In a case where your current supervisor already knows you are seeking new employment, by all means, feel free to list them as a reference. But in a normal scenario where you are trying to keep a tight lid on the fact that you are job hunting, it is 100 percent okay—and expected—that you'll leave off any contacts affiliated with your current employer.

Even worse than listing coworkers as references is when candidates choose friends and family members. Your best friend since third grade might say the nicest things about you, but he can't speak to what you're like as an employee, and even if he could, he's biased because he's your friend. Employers know that they'll never get an objective opinion by talking to your Uncle Joe or your college roommate. They will also be more likely to question your judgment if you include personal contacts on a professional reference list.

The only exception is if you are asked for "character references" or "personal references." Different ball game. The point of a character reference is to get a sense of who you are as a person, your values, and so on. A friend who has known you forever, a family member, a neighbor, a member of your church, a sports coach, a friend from a charity that you're involved in outside of work—all of these are great examples of good character or personal references.

Professional references are the most common type to be asked for, but some employers will want both professional and character references. It is best to be prepared for either scenario, and only furnish exactly what is requested.

KEEP YOUR REFERENCES INFORMED

This is one of the most common-sense rules, but people fail to do it all the time: Always ask for someone's permission before listing them as a reference! You can say something as simple as, "I really enjoyed working with you, and I think that your insights would help prospective employers get a real sense of my skills and capabilities. Do you mind if I list you as a reference?" Obtain each person's explicit permission.

Making the ask is a matter of proper respect, but it also serves you. If you have asked for someone's permission and given them a proper heads-up that they may be called, that person is far more likely to be pleasant and helpful and say nice things when a hiring manager reaches out to them.

> Always obtain someone's explicit permission before listing them as a reference.

Nothing starts a reference call off on the wrong foot quite like when the person has absolutely no idea why they are being called. When they say, "Wait, who are you calling to ask me about?" Or, "Oh, I had no idea he gave out my phone number," that certainly makes things awkward. It also won't reflect well on the candidate, who now comes across as disorganized and uncouth.

Don't let this be you. It is so unprofessional and easily avoidable. Before assuming anything, have the respect for people to ask them upfront if they are willing to be a reference for you.

A second courtesy is to provide your references with a heads-up as interviews are progressing. Especially if you are particularly excited about an opportunity, tell the people on your reference list, "I am in the final round of interviews with ABC Corp. I really love the company and am hoping to work there. You may be receiving a call from their HR department soon, so I just wanted to let you know in advance."

This way your references will know to expect the call. The advance notice may also prompt them to take extra care in answering the caller's questions thoroughly and thoughtfully because they know how important the opportunity is to you. Be sure to give them the name of the employer, the position you are being considered for, and any other pertinent details. Maybe even give them a quick synopsis of why you think you're a great fit. Keep it brief and sincere. It's a courteous thing to do, and it could increase your chances of being selected.

CHOOSE WISELY

That leads me to another crucial point that you may never have considered: not everyone you ask may truly want to be a reference for you. Maybe they are super busy, or they feel they don't know you well enough. Perhaps they don't want to do it because they have a negative opinion of you that you're not even aware of.

If you make the ask and get the sense that the other person is hesitating even one iota, *leave them off your list*. If there is anything worse than an awkward reference call, it's a negative one. A bad reference is serious and will almost certainly cost you job offers.

ou think, "Oh, that'll never happen to me," think again.
other little-known secret is that negative references
are given *all the time*. References tend to be quite honest,
for better or for worse, especially if the employer calling
them is savvy enough to ask insightful questions and dig
for deeper answers.

If a reference vouches for someone who doesn't deserve
it, they will look like a liar (or unprofessional themselves)
if and when that candidate screws up at their next job.
The HR manager will think, "Why did so-and-so give this
guy such a good reference? He's terrible." This is why
references tend to be pretty upfront and honest. Their
own reputation and credibility are on the line.

Here's a common example: A candidate tells a hiring
manager that she was laid off from a previous employer
and lists a supervisor from that company on her reference list. When the reference is contacted and asked to
verify dates of employment and why the candidate left,
the reference says, "The dates are correct, but she was
fired, and here's why..."

As if it's not bad enough that the candidate lied about
getting fired, now the door is wide open for the hiring
manager to pry into an obviously negative situation. In
a case like this, the candidate's chances of getting hired
have just been ruined.

Reference calls are usually conducted by HR professionals and recruiters, all of whom do this for a living and are skilled at getting people to level with them. A common question for a reference to be asked is, "Would you hire this person back?" Most of the time, they will say yes. But many times, the answer is no. And once they've said no, the next obvious question is, "Why not?" From there, the conversation is headed nowhere positive.

From my personal experience, reference checks result in a positive reflection of a candidate about 75 percent of the time. The other 25 percent, they are downright awful or questionable enough to devastate a candidate's chances at a job they otherwise might have been offered.

So, choose your references with extreme care and caution. You need to have your finger on the pulse of who will sing your praises and who might not. Negative is obviously bad, but neutral is not good. You want genuine enthusiasm. Always go for your biggest fans. In your heart, you'll know who they are. A good rule of thumb is that if you have to question whether or not someone will give you a good review, something is not right. Do not gamble with unknowns here.

GUT CHECK TIME: YOUR OPINION MATTERS TOO

By this point in the process, hopefully you're taking

the decision about whether or not you want to work for the employer as seriously as the employer is taking the decision whether or not to hire you. As hard as they are scrutinizing you (and the other remaining candidates), you should be scrutinizing them. After all, there is a strong chance that you'll be receiving an offer. Do you want it? Is this the company you want to work for? Is the job itself right for you?

Are you truly excited and hoping for that offer? Or are you hesitant? Either way, do some soul searching. Refer to those self-reflection exercises you did way back when you started this process. Is this opportunity in alignment with your needs and desires? Or have you gotten off track?

If you have lingering questions that need to be answered, now is the time to ask. In order to know whether or not you want a job, you certainly need to feel that you have all the information: a very clear idea of the position, the expectations, the team you'd be working with, the company culture, and so on. If a lack of information is giving you pause, figure out what is at the root of your uncertainty. You should have a solid rapport with at least one person, if not more, within the company. Reach out and ask any remaining questions that are on your mind. Now is the time to get clear, before an offer is extended.

Once you have all the information, it's time to decide

firmly. Is this the job you want? Or should you move on?

IT'S TIME TO LET THIS ONE GO: HOW DO YOU DO IT?

If you have that sinking feeling in your gut that something isn't right, it isn't. Your intuition is signaling you to move on from the opportunity. Should you just forge ahead and see how things shake out, even if you know deep down that this opportunity isn't for you? No, you shouldn't, for all of the reasons we've discussed in the previous chapters. It's not your goal to land any job, it's your goal to land the *right* job. And this isn't it. You need to pass.

This can be a difficult conclusion to arrive at, especially after progressing so far in the process. Here you are, having invested time, energy, and emotion for weeks or even months, and you've connected with a company that really likes you and is probably going to make you an offer. It's disheartening to know that it was all for nothing. You might also be feeling guilty for having "wasted" people's time up to this point.

It is common for one side in a hiring equation to get excited about a match, while the other side just doesn't feel it. The employer might be thinking, "This candidate is exactly what we've been looking for. He's perfect."

Meanwhile, you might be saying to yourself, "This does not feel right."

Maybe you don't want to relocate after all, or you aren't thrilled about the culture. Maybe you met the manager and thought, "I'm not sure how well we would work together." Perhaps you're very ambitious and want to move up, but you learned that the company doesn't have a good track record of promoting from within. Or it could be something someone said during the interview process turned you off, and you haven't been able to get past it.

As soon as you know that an opportunity is not right for you, it's best to speak up and pull yourself out of the running. The employer probably has another strong candidate or two in the mix at this stage, and the last thing they want to do is make an offer to someone who is going to turn it down. Allow them to redirect their energy toward the remaining candidates who do genuinely want the job. It's okay to say no. It really does happen all the time, for all kinds of reasons.

It's time to let this one go. How exactly should you do it?

Never "ghost" an employer. Sadly, it happens all the time, and it is beyond unprofessional and rude. Ghosting accomplishes nothing positive and will only leave a bad lasting impression that could come back to haunt you (no pun intended) in the long run.

When removing yourself from consideration, have the intestinal fortitude to have an actual conversation with a human being. Think about whom you've had the closest relationship with and dealt with most directly throughout the process—an HR associate, a department head, etc. Then, pick up the phone. Do not send an email—or worse, a text message. Call the person and explain to them that you are pulling yourself out of the running.

It is *not* necessary to be very specific here. You do owe them the decency of a conversation, but you are not obligated to disclose your actual reasons for moving on. Your responsibility is really more about honoring the human connection and conveying, "I really appreciate the time, energy, and interest that you've invested in seeing if we were the right fit for one another, but I've come to the conclusion that this isn't the right opportunity for me."

Most likely, the hiring team will be disappointed, but they will understand. They will respect your professionalism and, on some level, will feel relieved. They'll know that they just avoided potentially hiring someone who would have been dissatisfied in the role and that they dodged a bullet. They'll be thinking, "That's too bad, but better we know now."

WHAT TO DO IF THIS IS "THE ONE"

If your enthusiasm level is still high and you genuinely want this job, the best thing you can do now is make sure the company knows how you feel. We've already talked a bit about the power of enthusiasm, and that is never more meaningful than in these final stages of the hiring process.

In this final phase, convey interest through your words *and* your actions. If the employer asks you back for additional interviews, schedule them quickly and show up on time looking fresh and happy to be there. Fill out assessments as soon as you are asked. Provide strong references. Knock projects out of the park, and go the extra mile making sure that everything is perfect. Ask good questions as they come to mind. All of these actions show the hiring team that you want the position and are right there with them. You should also say, sincerely and bluntly, "I really hope to work here. I want this job."

These are the things that will set you apart from your competition, at a time when every little detail counts. Remember, you are under a microscope now and any action you take (or don't), as well as any impression you leave can be the difference between getting hired and losing out.

As badly as they may want the job, I see many candidates get frustrated during this final phase. Maybe they are irritated that the process has dragged on much longer than expected, or they are taking it personally that the employer is really torn between a couple of final candidates. They want to feel wanted. When they don't receive a quick offer, they overthink and question everything. Their enthusiasm starts to wane. Please do your absolute best not to let yourself get down. Getting sucked into a depressed or negative state won't feel good or do you any favors. Plus, the employer will pick up on it, and it could cost you an offer.

You've come so far by this point. If you still want the job, keep your energy up, be positive, and give it your best right up until the end.

KEY POINTS IN THIS CHAPTER

Hiring processes can be lengthy, with multiple hoops to jump through. Be patient and remember that each phase has a purpose.

Complete the final steps as directed, promptly and thoughtfully. You are almost at the end, so don't lose steam or momentum now.

Select your references wisely and furnish them only upon request.

If you feel that a position or employer isn't the right fit for you, say so as soon as you know for sure so that both sides can move on.

If you feel that a position is the right fit for you, make sure the employer knows it! Enthusiasm goes a long way, and they want to hire someone who truly wants the job.

Chapter Six

SO, THEY MADE YOU AN OFFER— NOW WHAT?

You've made it to the end and your efforts have paid off. You have a formal offer in hand! You should be proud.

When you receive the proposal, emotion is likely to take over, at least initially. Again, it's great to be wanted. But before you get caught up in the euphoria and excitement, try to stay cool and think rationally. Receiving an offer is not quite the end of the road; the hiring process extends through the actual *acceptance* of an offer. And you're not quite there yet.

Keeping your emotions at bay and staying objective is easier said than done, I know. You want it to work out. Trust me, the employer wants it to work out, too. By the time the offer letter is created and presented to you, the hiring team has been through a long and arduous process of evaluation and selection. They have done a ton of diligence and have chosen you. The company is already mentally preparing for you to join their team. Their best-case scenario is that you verbally commit, return the signed letter, and give your two weeks' notice to your current employer pretty much immediately. You're on the two-yard line now. This part should be simple, right?

Not so fast.

There is a *lot* that can happen between your receiving that letter and showing up on your first day with a new employer.

Do not let games, arrogance, or silly mistakes derail the train now. This phase needs to be handled delicately and thoughtfully to achieve the ideal result—a deal that both sides can feel good about. This chapter will address frequently asked questions involving the offer stage. It will also walk you through some of the most common scenarios and how best to navigate them.

VERBAL VS. WRITTEN OFFERS

An offer may initially come to you in the form of a written letter, or it could be presented verbally. Many companies prefer to discuss the terms of an offer over the phone (or sometimes even in person) before putting anything in writing. They do this to ensure that everyone is on the same page. Drawing up the formal paperwork can be time consuming. They may not want to take that step until they know for sure that a candidate will be accepting, and what the official terms will be. Other companies put everything in writing upfront, without much discussion beforehand.

The level of communication and rapport you've had with the hiring manager to this point may also dictate how the offer is delivered. If the two of you have gotten close throughout the application process, she may call you with a congratulatory heads-up before a formal letter is sent. Another factor here is how in depth the discussions have previously been regarding salary expectations. If you've already communicated your comp expectation earlier in the process and the hiring team knows that the number is non-negotiable, they may be more likely to send you the letter without any discussion upfront because, well, there isn't much to talk about.

The moral of the story is, be prepared for either verbal or written offers. In my experience, it's about 50/50 which method employers prefer. You're very likely to encounter both scenarios during your search.

SALARY CONSIDERATIONS

The key component in any offer letter is the proposed salary. Most candidates zero in on that right away, and for good reason. Compensation is important and always a major factor in a candidate's decision to accept or reject any offer. But is it wise to ask for more money?

TO NEGOTIATE OR NOT TO NEGOTIATE?

Whether or not you negotiate salary should depend on what conversations have already occurred about compensation, and how the offer compares to what was discussed. If there has already been frank candor about the company's budget and your expectations, both sides should be essentially on the same page by this point. If the offer matches the number you asked for, all the negotiation has already been done. Accept it. If the salary proposed is not what you expected, less than what you are comfortable accepting, or lower than you were led to believe it might be, you'll probably want to take a shot at getting the number up.

Some employers will be open to negotiation and others will not. Many companies like to present their "best and final" upfront, to eliminate any uncomfortable back and forth. You probably won't know which category a particular employer falls into. If you do decide to negotiate, be prepared for either response.

If the salary number isn't quite right, but everything else about the opportunity is exactly what you want, you may ask yourself, "Can I live with this salary?" When it comes down to it, your quality of life and your happiness are important, too, and not everything can be measured in zeros. I sometimes see candidates take pay cuts for improvements in culture and job satisfaction, or quality of life. Trading a two-hour commute for a ten-minute one just might make a reduction in pay palatable. Massive improvements in one area can make other components of an offer acceptable.

If the number is close enough to what you hoped for, you're probably smart to just say yes. If you try to negotiate higher, you may get what you ask for, but you're also running the risk of rubbing the hiring team the wrong way. It's also possible that they could rescind the offer if they feel you've pushed them too far. If you're planning to join the company no matter what, it's probably not worth the risk of starting off on the wrong foot.

Sometimes both sides are just too far apart on salary to make it work. Or they might be very close but stuck on their individual numbers and unwilling to budge or meet in the middle. If an offer comes your way and the compensation is just not acceptable to you, there is nothing wrong with walking away. I hate to see someone stay in a miserable job versus taking one they might love over a small amount of money, but it's also true that you should not sell yourself short for an unreasonably low offer. Only you can determine what feels right to you and what does not. The final decision is always in your hands, and yours alone.

WHAT IF SALARY WASN'T BROUGHT UP UNTIL NOW?

Sometimes the topic of salary never comes up until the offer stage. It's not outside the realm of possibility that you may get a surprise phone call from the hiring manager saying something like, "We'd really like to make you an offer. Can you tell me your comp expectation?" This can really catch people off guard, and it's easy to see why. How do you respond?

My advice is the same, regardless of when in the process salary is addressed: just be honest. Again, you are never required to disclose your current salary, but you are welcome to do so if you feel comfortable or want to for any reason. Regardless, you should be very upfront about your salary *expectation*. You could say something like, "My current salary is $85,000. I'm really excited about this opportunity and would be willing to make a lateral move, but I cannot accept anything less than what I am making now." Or, "I'm excited about this opportunity, but I need an increase in salary to justify making a change. My expectation is $100,000, or as close to it as possible."

Just be cautious not to gamble too hard, because asking for an outrageous number can turn things sour quickly. Be realistic, be honest, and always remain gracious. Game playing never works. Better to be direct and put all your cards on the table.

Never dodge the salary question when asked. Never, ever, ever. It is an instant turnoff to an employer. Candidates who keep their number close to the vest and say things like, "I would rather not disclose that," or "Well, what do you think I am worth?" or "Just make me an offer," will likely see that strategy backfire. Not only are they running the risk of seeming disingenuous, they are also leaving the door wide open to be lowballed if the employer does extend them an offer. Trust me, it's always better to be upfront. Let the deal come together if it's meant to.

PROOF OF SALARY

It's rare, but some companies will ask candidates for a copy of their W-2, pay stub, or other documentation to verify employment and proof of income. At the time of this writing, while there is no federal law that prohibits this, some states do not allow it. If you are asked to produce any of these documents, whether you do so or not is up to you. Some candidates see it as an invasion of privacy and prefer not to disclose. Others have no issue with the request, having an attitude of, "I've been honest up to this point and have nothing to hide, who cares if they see my W-2."

Now, there are some cases where I have *encouraged* my candidates to provide W-2 information to potential employers, whether the information was requested of them or not. Depending on the situation, you may want to do the same. Why?

Let's say you're making $95,000 and you get an offer from a potential employer that is lower, say $90,000. You've already told them that your expectation is $100,000. This may be a good opportunity for you to provide proof of income in order to negotiate the salary you want and deserve. It's possible to do this in a gracious way by saying, "I really want to join your team, but you are asking me to take a pay cut. I am not comfortable going backward at this stage in my career. Here is my proof of income. If you are able to at least match it, I would be glad to accept. I sincerely hope we can make this work." In this case you are not being difficult, you're sticking up for yourself. Totally understandable, especially if you've already made your salary expectations clear.

ONLINE DATA

Some candidates negotiate salary by referencing online data. Perhaps they go to sites like Glassdoor.com or study industry surveys. I suppose information is never a bad thing, but be advised that whatever you find online may not always be accurate or relevant. Also, your experience level might not match the "average" person in your field. There are many variables. Research if you must and use the information you uncover as a rough guide, but try not to get too wrapped up in salary data you come across online.

Whatever you do, never throw online data in an employer's face. I have heard stories of candidates saying, "You offered me $75,000, and I know that's $10,000 more than what I asked for, but I did a little market research last night and realized that the going rate for a position like this is actually $90,000, so I think that's what I deserve."

I promise you, if you do this, the employer will be irritated at best, and will rescind the offer at worst. Put yourself in their shoes: here they are, delivering a very generous offer at $10,000 above what you asked for, only to be met with totally unexpected pushback.

If you put credence in online data and feel it is important to consider, then do your research long before you are asked about your personal salary expectation. Then, factor the data into whatever number you state as your expectation.

Be aware that many employers have the attitude that market salary data is irrelevant. When they are told by a candidate, "This is what the market is paying," the employer's knee-jerk response is most likely to be, "That may be what you found on the internet, but *this* is our budget." Maybe next year the hiring manager will approach the executive team about rethinking compensation structure and budgets for certain roles, but generally not in this moment, for one specific person.

Industry standards (if there even is such a thing) rarely factor into what an employer will offer. That business owner or hiring manager is concerned with only two things: (1) their budget and (2) the candidate's salary requirement. Everything else is irrelevant.

> That business owner or hiring manager is concerned with only two things: (1) their budget and (2) the candidate's salary requirement. Everything else is irrelevant.

BEYOND SALARY: OTHER NEGOTIABLES

As important as salary is, there is much more to a job than just compensation. I always encourage my candidates to maintain a perspective broader than salary alone. When you started this process, your job search probably wasn't entirely about money to begin with. Salary is just one piece; don't let it become your sole focus and cause you to lose perspective on other components.

Evaluate opportunities in terms of the big picture, with special emphasis on what is most important to you, personally. Once again, go back to your self-reflection exercises and the list of non-negotiables you created at the beginning of your search. With an offer letter in hand, you now have every piece to the puzzle. It's time to take a hard look at this new opportunity *as a whole* before you decide whether you will accept or reject.

Sometimes candidates will be happy with the proposed salary, but something else will prevent them from feeling excited about accepting the offer. If this is you, identify what is giving you pause and see if those pieces can be negotiated, fixed, or addressed.

Negotiations very often involve aspects of an opportunity that have nothing to do with salary. Candidates might say, "I accept the salary, but can we discuss something else?" If salary is non-negotiable for the employer, it is possible to turn a so-so offer into something far more enticing by negotiating other components. In fact, it's common for companies to sweeten the pot with non-monetary perks. They can be flexible on these items, since salary budgets are often set in stone, but miscellaneous benefits are not. It is easier for the employer to justify giving someone a few special perks on their way in the door than it would be to pay a salary that is way out of whack.

> The odds of successfully negotiating non-salary related perks are in your favor.

Little-known fact: the odds of successfully negotiating non-salary related perks are in your favor. At this stage, employers want to get a deal done. If a candidate tells them that they have a "yes" on the salary amount if they can do X and Y, the employer will usually fold pretty easily. It is much easier for them to make it work at this stage, as opposed to starting the process all over again. So read this section carefully, and don't be afraid to use it to your advantage in scenarios where negotiating salary isn't an option. I'll quickly run through some of the most popular examples.

VACATION TIME

This one speaks for itself. Vacation policies vary. Let's say a company offers three weeks' vacation to all employees, regardless of how long they have worked there. They have made you an offer. With your current employer, you have accrued five weeks of vacation because you have worked there for so long. You're willing to take a lateral salary if the new employer will work with you on the issue of the vacation time. Perhaps you explain the situation and ask them to meet you halfway (four weeks of vacation time). They could say yes or no, but it's a fair ask.

REMOTE WORK

The benefit of working from home is becoming more and more widespread. Frankly, most employers aren't crazy about their employees working off-site. But it's becoming increasingly common in today's world, especially in large cities where traffic can be horrendous. Employees don't want to lose three hours of their day sitting in traffic, and employers don't want to lose out on great people over the same complication. So, they are apt to negotiate a flex or remote work schedule.

Your luck with this will depend largely on your industry. If you do customer service and all you need to do your job effectively is a cell phone and a laptop, there's a pretty easy case to be made for working remotely. On the other hand, if you work in property management it'll be impossible to do your job effectively without being at the physical location to interact with tenants, oversee capital improvement projects, and so on. Professional services firms tend to be more traditional, whereas startups and more creative industries might be looser with these policies. Use your common sense in determining what might be an appropriate ask, versus what might not.

If the company wants employees in the office five days per week, but your commute is going to be awful, maybe you ask to work from home only on Wednesdays to break up your week. Or ask if you can alter your schedule slightly (come in an hour early, leave an hour early) to avoid the worst of the traffic.

SHORT-TERM GROWTH

Some candidates will accept lower salaries if they have a short-term trajectory and opportunity for quick growth clearly mapped out. An employer might agree to a performance review in six months, at which point the candidate will be eligible for a bump in salary and title. This could satisfy both parties. The employer can bring in the candidate at a comfortable number, and the candidate walks in the door knowing that they have rapid growth opportunity if they prove themselves.

MISCELLANEOUS PERKS

There are many miscellaneous items up for negotiation, depending on the industry. Project managers in construction might ask for company vehicles. Hospitality professionals might ask for free dry cleaning. Salespeople who spend lots of time on the road might ask for a gas card to cover their transportation costs. Anyone working in a downtown area might request free parking. The list goes on and on. If you can think of anything reasonable that applies to your specific industry or role, don't be afraid to ask.

TIMING IS EVERYTHING

If you have a quirky or unusual non-negotiable that is personal to you, your best shot at effectively negotiating it is during the offer stage. Timing is everything, and you have far more negotiating power *after* an employer has decided that they like you and want you. If you bring up your request for extra vacation time or your desire for a flex schedule too early in the hiring process, you'll run the risk of being labeled high maintenance or demanding. If you save it for when the employer just wants to get a deal done, they'll be more likely to think, "He's the right guy for us, and what he's asking for isn't worth losing him over. Let's just say yes."

THE IMPORTANCE OF GRATITUDE

Whatever your feelings about the initial offer, it is so important to make a quick phone call to the hiring manager to say, "Thank you so much for this offer. I am really honored and grateful." Keep up that positive energy and momentum that we've talked about so many times.

THE CAT HOSPITAL

My firm recently recruited a woman for a mid-level human resources position. Her passion outside of work was animals, and she volunteered regularly at a cat hospital. This volunteer position was extremely important to her, and she expressed adamantly to us that she would not give it up. The trouble was, it required her to leave work a couple of hours early every Thursday to get to the facility for her shift. She absolutely would not work for any employer that wouldn't accommodate this schedule.

As the recruiter, I felt slightly ridiculous allowing a job to hinge on a cat hospital, but I could tell how important it was to her (and in a way, the whole thing was sort of endearing). The cat hospital was a non-negotiable for the candidate, and one that my client was going to need to accept if they wanted to hire her. I was confident that this woman was the right match for the job, and I went to bat for her.

I knew that we needed to be honest with the client about the issue but took a gamble and decided not to mention it upfront. I was confident that our odds of dealing with it (with a favorable outcome) would be better if we just went smoothly through the hiring process, and then worked it out at the end. I knew that my client would fall in love with this candidate, especially after struggling for so long to find someone with her exact qualifications. Sure enough, she flew through her interviews and had an offer in her hands one week later. That was when I took a deep breath and said to myself, "Okay, time to tackle this cat hospital thing." (It sounds funny now, but it was really stressful at the time!)

I called the client and explained, "Kate is thrilled to accept this offer, and it's the perfect fit for you both. She is so excited, and she wants to start in two weeks; congratulations! But here's the thing. She needs to leave a little early every Thursday. I know you guys are rigid about your schedules, but she's willing to come in early on those days to make up the hours. Can we just make this happen?" By that time, the company was so ready to be done with the whole process that they rolled over and said, "No problem." I know if I'd had the same conversation with them prior to the first interview, they would have thought, "Ugh, we don't do high-maintenance employees here. Pass."

Communication after an offer is critical in keeping the employer from getting worried or irritated, so don't leave them high and dry wondering what you are thinking. Plus, if you've communicated to them that you received the offer and are excited about it, they'll be more understanding and less nervous if you truly do need a day or two to sleep on it.

No employer wants to feel like a new hire is limping over the finish line. If you propose marriage to someone and they say, "I really love you, but I need some time to think about it," that wouldn't exactly make you feel very good, would it? The company wants you jumping in with both feet. In the event that some component of the offer does need to be negotiated at the final stage, an employer will be far more likely to work with you on those points if they have reassurance that you truly want to be a part of their team.

Also, never play hard to get when an employer puts a bona

fide offer on the table. I have seen candidates try to leverage offers by claiming to have other offers on the table (whether they really do or not) to create the perception that they are in high demand. Candidates think they will have more negotiating power if the employer believes they are wanted by other companies. This strategy backfires every single time. *Do not do it.*

> Never play hard to get when an employer puts a bona fide offer on the table. This strategy backfires every single time.

Think of the marriage proposal example again. How would someone feel after proposing and getting the reaction, "Oh, thanks for the proposal, but I have a few other suitors chasing me as well. I can't commit until I know who is going to give me the biggest ring." Yuck, right? The person who proposed isn't going to fight harder for a yes. Instead they're going to think, "Screw this person, I can do better," and *they* will move on.

I have seen employers rescind offers under these circumstances dozens of times over the years. Playing hard to get is a horrible strategy. After making the employer sweat it, if you say no, you look like a jerk who wasted a lot of people's time. If you say yes, you've started off on the wrong foot. If you're still in limbo and hoping to make a few tweaks to the offer, you've just thrown away any negotiating power you otherwise might have had. In any scenario, you've lost. Be grateful and gracious, always.

ASK MORE QUESTIONS

After you've received an offer, it's okay to ask more questions. No one will fault you for your desire to gain greater clarity. As much as the company wants you to say yes, they also want you to make the right decision for you. Remember, they want employees who will be happy on their team long term. If you can't see yourself in a role (or in a company) for at least two years, you probably shouldn't accept. I know that time frame may seem somewhat arbitrary, but it's a good rule of thumb to avoid finding yourself just killing time until your next job search begins.

Not sure if you see the opportunity being a long-term fit? Time to ask more questions. Pick up the phone, call the hiring manager, and talk through what's on your mind. Approach them directly and say, "X, Y, and Z are hanging me up a bit. Can we discuss them more?"

Employers will be happy to get you the information you need and do what they can to clarify any unclear points. It's perfectly acceptable to gather more information before making a huge decision that will impact your career and your life.

Even the most diligent candidates who ask tons of questions throughout the process may get to the end and realize there are still a few stones unturned. With an offer now on the table, it's real. Candidates are hit with the reality of, "Oh, wow. I actually have to make this decision." It can be overwhelming and cause brand new questions to flood in. This is normal.

Common questions at this stage involve details about the health insurance plan and other benefits, or logistical matters like vacation time, hours, start date, and so on. Maybe something wasn't explained clearly during the interview process and you want to revisit that issue. Or perhaps there is a key person you never got to meet because they were away on vacation. That might leave you feeling like, "I can't accept until I've met this person and know for sure that we click."

Figure out where the holes are and do not leave them unaddressed. Shroud your questions in gratitude and enthusiasm and ask away. I recommend saying, "Could you please help me cover these last couple of bases before I say yes?" Believe me, the hiring team will be happy to oblige.

IT'S A YES! (ACCEPTING AN OFFER)

If the offer is the right opportunity for you and you're

going to say yes, do it as soon as you know. Do not hesitate or drag out the acceptance. Never say, "I need a day or two to think about it," for no good reason.

This company is officially going to be your new employer. The best way to start off on the right foot with them is to accept the offer right away and with enthusiasm. Their ideal scenario is that they hear from you same day, saying how thrilled you are to accept their offer. They put a lot of thought into selecting you as their final candidate, so give them a response that will affirm their choice.

Now, if you are truly unsure, it is acceptable to take some time. You won't have a lot of it, but generally twenty-four to forty-eight hours is considered reasonable. Some offer letters will state a deadline for providing your answer. If there is a set window, respect it, and do not take up the full time you've been allotted unless you absolutely must.

Here's the problem with hesitating: It makes the employer nervous. It also causes them to question why you aren't giving them an enthusiastic, immediate yes. Candidates will often know they are going to say yes, but they delay replying for a day or two before formally accepting. I think they are trying to avoid seeming impulsive or like they haven't thought it through. It's silly when you think about it—how could the decision be impulsive when you've been analyzing it from every angle for weeks (or even months) throughout the hiring process?

There's no sense causing the employer to wonder, "Why does he need to think about it? What is going on?" The last thing you want is for them to question or rethink whether you are the right hire. There is also a part of them that's thinking, "If this guy turns us down, we need to start the search all over again. We can't afford to waste any time." From this perspective, it's easier to understand why employers are anxious to know where you stand, sooner than later.

A WORD ABOUT RELOCATIONS

For certain (generally senior level) openings, companies will consider out-of-market candidates and ask the successful one to relocate.

If the position requires a candidate to relocate, it is assumed that they will probably need some extra time to come to a final decision. Upon receiving the offer, the candidate might tell the employer, "I'm so thrilled, and I appreciate the offer. I just need a few days to work out some of the logistics and talk everything over with my family." Especially in cases where a relocating candidate would be uprooting a spouse or children, employers tend to be very understanding.

Families need to consider everything from schools to real estate to cost of living and so much more. It's a lot. Yes, it's true that they have been thinking through all of these things throughout the process, but once that piece of paper is in front of them it takes on a whole new level of "real."

If you ever find yourself being considered for a job in a new city, do everyone (yourself included) a big favor and research the area as thoroughly as you can early in the interview process. Ask yourself, "Could I really see myself living here?" And if applicable, "Could I really see my family living here?"

These are questions you should be asking yourself before you even submit your resume for jobs in different locations. Once a company shows interest, it's easy to get caught up in the flattery of being pursued, so much so that you might lose sight of the bigger picture. As exciting as an opportunity may be, and a great fit in many ways, if you're not willing to uproot and move, you run the risk of colossally wasting everyone's time. Do not wait until the eleventh hour to figure out if accepting the job is a viable option due to its location.

YOU'RE HIRED!

When formally accepting, return the signed offer letter

and follow up with a phone call. It's nice to make one final human connection to confirm they received your letter and say thank you one more time. During that conversation, you'll also want to make a decision about your start date and any other check-the-box items that need to be dealt with—a background check, drug test, additional paperwork, and so on.

Once you formally say yes, you're in. You're part of the family. This is your new employer! *Success*! Go in with a great attitude and don't look back.

The hope is that you'll be there, happily, for many years to come. If you've done your diligence up to this point, odds are that you've made a great decision and this opportunity will be well suited to you. Embrace it and give it all you've got.

IT'S A NO (REJECTING AN OFFER)

Sometimes, you just have to say no. If an opportunity isn't right or the offer isn't something that you are comfortable accepting, you'll need to decline.

When turning down an offer, keep it classy in every aspect. Timeliness shows respect. Tell the employer as soon as possible so that they can move on. They may have a second-choice candidate on the back burner that they don't want to lose, and the sooner they can reach out to that person, the better their chances of not losing two top candidates.

A one-line email saying, "I cannot accept," or "Thank you for the consideration, but it's a no," is *not* an appropriate conclusion to a long and intense interview process. Not responding at all is even worse (yes, people do it all the time). I know it's uncomfortable, but pick up the phone and call the hiring manager directly. You are a professional adult; do the right thing and initiate a one-on-one conversation.

When you deliver the bad news, you're likely to hear something to the effect of, "That's really disappointing. Why are you declining the offer?" This question can be a little tricky, and you'll need to give some thought to your answer beforehand. I recommend being sufficiently specific without "oversharing."

Think about what you would want to hear from a company that rejected you. You wouldn't want to know every little nitpicky thing they might not have liked, right? Being criticized to that extent would just feel hurtful and over the top. But I bet you *would* want to know of any major deal-breakers, so you could improve your performance next time and leave this opportunity behind thinking, "Okay, I understand what went wrong." Same concept applies when you are turning down an employer.

Do not be overly generic ("It just wasn't the right fit"), but do not delve into every gory detail about what you didn't like about the company, the people, and so on. Condense your reasoning into one clear, succinct nugget that helps the hiring manager put this to bed and move on. "I just cannot relocate my family." "I cannot take a reduction in pay." "I feel that the responsibilities are too lateral." Or, "I did not feel I would mesh well with the existing team." These are all good examples.

> When rejecting an offer, condense your reasoning into one clear, succinct nugget that helps the hiring manager put this to bed and move on.

You'll also want to ensure that you part ways on the best note possible. You never know where a relationship can go in the future. Perhaps you turned down the job because you felt that the responsibilities were too lateral for you, and you want your next move to be a step up. If you leave the hiring manager with a positive impression, she might call you a few months down the road when a more senior-level position opens up. On the other hand, if you handle things poorly as you part ways, she will note in her files (and to the entire HR team) not to contact you again in the future.

Lastly, never underestimate the power of relationships and referrals. HR people know other HR people. Company owners and executives socialize and network with other owners and executives. If you've made a good impression on someone, the next time they are at a cocktail party and hear another person say, "I'm looking to hire X, do you know of anyone?" your name just might get passed along. You never know where your next opportunity will come from. But if you've burned a bridge somewhere along the way, you can bet you'll attract fewer of them.

SAYING GOODBYE TO YOUR CURRENT EMPLOYER

Once you've accepted a new position, it's time to notify your current employer that you'll be leaving. This is more uncomfortable for some people than others. For those who have been with a company for a long time or have developed particularly close relationships with supervisors and coworkers, giving notice can be much harder. But it's something that you must do in order to embark on your new adventure. Bite the bullet and just get it done.

Before you resign, take a deep breath and remind yourself of all the reasons why you made this decision. Stand absolutely firm. Have the mindset that you will be kind and respectful but matter-of-fact. You are there to communicate your decision and come up with a plan for your exit. Nothing more, nothing less.

These conversations usually go one of two ways. There are the employers who will say, "Sorry to see you go," and immediately shift gears, beginning to plan for the transition without much discussion. Then there are the employers who will bombard you with questions like, "Why are you leaving? Why didn't you tell us that you were unhappy? Where are you going?!"

Here's what you need to know: You are *not*, under any circumstances, obligated to answer these uncomfortable questions. It is nobody's business where you are going, why you are leaving, and why the new opportunity is a better one for you. Keep that information private. Besides, answering the questions only opens the door for your manager to grill you further and invites a debate which won't end well.

> When giving notice, you are *not*, under any circumstances, obligated to answer questions about where you are going or why you are leaving.

You're trying to leave on a classy note, and it's pretty much impossible to do that when you're engaging in a discussion about why you're leaving for an opportunity that is better. Unless you have an amazing supervisor who is truly supportive, wants to understand exactly where you are coming from, and won't take it personally (rare!), engaging in much dialogue here is a bad idea. You'll just go in circles, and no one will leave the conversation feeling warm and fuzzy.

HOW MUCH NOTICE?

Candidates frequently ask me how much notice they should give. This is always a little tricky because you're dancing a fine line now between appeasing your new employer (who probably wants you to start as soon as possible) and doing right by your soon-to-be old employer (who probably wants to keep you on as long as possible while they plan for the transition). Do the best you can here, while keeping in mind that if the two are in conflict, you're better off keeping your new employer happy. By accepting their offer, you've already declared a shifting loyalty.

You are never obligated to give more than two weeks' notice, so do not let an employer guilt you into staying for any more than that. Likewise, do not let a new employer pressure you into giving any less notice. You want to be fair to all parties, and if there is any question in your mind about the best course of action, just tell everyone your plan is two weeks. Even if one side is irritated because they were hoping it would be more or less, they won't hold it against you. Two weeks is standard and perfectly professional.

If you feel you need to stay longer to wrap up specific

projects, trust your instincts. I see this happen often with senior-level employees whose positions are more complex and time consuming to fill. Likewise, if your job is very project based and you feel like you'd be leaving your ex-employer in a bad spot unless you tie up some loose ends, do what you need to do. Flexibility within reason is fine as long as there's an agreed-upon time frame. But again, there is never an obligation to stay longer than two weeks.

Occasionally, I will hear a candidate say, "This company has been awful to me, so I'm out of there in one week," (or sometimes less!) They have such a bad taste for their current employer that they're tempted to give little to no notice at all, purely out of spite. Don't do this.

First, it's totally unprofessional. Second, your soon-to-be new employer will see this and wonder, "Is this person going to treat my company this way if and when they leave me someday?" It's not a good look. Regardless of how bad an experience may have been, take the high road and offer the standard two-week notice.

KEEP YOUR EXIT CLASSY

As tempting as it may be to go rogue on your way out the door or tell your supervisor all the horrible things you have felt for years, resist the temptation. Behave in a way that is beyond reproach, even if it's not necessarily what they deserve. Being rude or unprofessional just gives a former boss or colleague a reason to think negatively of you, and they could easily share that story with others in the industry. Why give them any ammo? Rising above it will serve you well, both now and in the future. Reputation matters, so take yours seriously.

In some cases, giving notice could cause you to get "walked," which means your employment will be terminated immediately and you'll be escorted out of the building. If this happens to you, do not be offended. A company may walk an outgoing employee for many reasons, none of which are personal. For example, they may worry that you are going to work for a competitor, and they can't risk you having further access to certain information. They may just not want to pay you for another two weeks. Whatever the case, it's fine. Remember, you left them, so they have a right to feel a certain way. They also need to do what they deem necessary to protect the company's best interest.

If you get walked, you have a couple of options. First, you can enjoy your two weeks off. Take a trip, chill out, enjoy your family, whatever. Regroup, recharge, and get ready to take on your new job. Of course, many people don't want to go two weeks without a paycheck. If that's you, your second option is to call your new employer, explain to them what happened, and ask if you can shift your start date sooner. They will usually say yes. In fact, they'll probably be thrilled to get you on board even sooner than expected.

DEALING WITH A COUNTEROFFER

I hate counteroffers. You should, too. They may sound great and exciting, but they are almost always the start of an ugly situation. Some candidates enter into their resignation meeting hoping for a counter, thinking they can use it to leverage their position and hedge their bets. If they receive one, they may present it to their potential new employer in hopes of getting them to sweeten the original offer. The candidate may also use the counter as justification to not make a move after all (maybe it was attractive enough it convinced them to stay put). Either way, these situations are messy and rarely end well.

If you "shop" your counteroffer by showing it to the company trying to hire you, they will be colossally annoyed. They will think, "This person already told us the salary he was looking for, we matched it, and now he wants to play games? No way." The relationship has just been soured. Your reliability and credibility are now in question, and that's a terrible place to be.

Is it possible that the new employer will roll over and

say, "Well, maybe this candidate is worth more, we'll increase our offer"? I mean, anything is *possible*, but I don't think I've ever seen this happen in all my years in the hiring industry. What I *have* seen countless times over is employers rescinding offers under these conditions.

On the flip side, let's say you accept the counteroffer and stay with your original employer. Believe it or not, this can be an even greater risk. Maybe you accept the counter because you are promised the world about things getting better. Your employer offers you more money, more flexibility, whatever the case may be. It goes without saying that you've permanently burned a bridge with the potential future employer. But, even worse, you have also let the cat out of the bag with your current employer that you were so unhappy in your position that you were out job hunting—and doing it so seriously that you got an offer. When the next round of layoffs comes, or when someone more loyal or less expensive surfaces, where do you think you'll be? Probably out of a job altogether, kicking yourself and wondering how you got there.

I have never heard anyone say, "I accepted a counteroffer and stayed—best decision of my career." It just doesn't happen, folks.

My firm worked with four candidates this past year alone who received counteroffers from their current employer and, against our advice, decided to accept them and stay. In every single one of those cases, those candidates expressed to my team months later that they regretted the decision. They also had something else in common. *None of their employers delivered on the promises they made when convincing them to stay.*

These candidates opted to give their employer a second chance because they were sold a bill of goods about things getting better, which never happened. Even if they received raises, the financial gain wasn't enough to make up for the other negative circumstances. All four of these people circled back saying, "I can't believe I took that counteroffer," and "Does that client of yours still have any openings? Do you think they would reconsider me?" The answer was a resounding no, four times over. Once something like this happens with a candidate, in the eyes of an employer, there's no rewinding the clock. It's done.

So when your boss invites you into a meeting after you've given notice, brace yourself for a counteroffer. Hold your ground, refuse to accept, and bring yourself mentally back to the reason you started a job search in the first place. (Hint: it was because you weren't happy!)

A LITTLE *ME* TIME?

What about taking an extra few days off between jobs to relax and regroup? There's nothing inherently wrong with it, so long as your new employer is okay with your proposed time frame. Whether you want to go to Maui or just enjoy a short staycation, do what you need to do, and keep it discreet. There is no need to explain the details of your plans. It's fine to say, "Do you mind if I delay my start for a few days to deal with a couple of personal matters?"

Candidates will often say they need three weeks between accepting the offer and actually starting the new job. They rarely explain why, but everyone knows it's because they're looking to put their feet up for a little while in between jobs. Regardless, employers will usually say it's no problem. A few days is not a big deal in the grand scheme of things. Anything within the two- to three-week time frame for a transition is considered reasonable.

Be aware that anything much beyond two weeks, and definitely three, will start to put the new employer on edge. Believe it or not, no-shows do happen, and they are a nightmare scenario for obvious reasons. Don't push your luck by extending start dates too far out. Be respectful of the fact that the employer wants to get this position filled, and you in the seat, as quickly as possible. And if you negotiate a little "me time," it's probably best to keep the pool bar selfies off social media.

HOLD FIRM, ELIZABETH

Elizabeth was a candidate I worked with last year, and a shining example of how best to handle a difficult situation with a soon-to-be-ex employer.

My team recruited Elizabeth for a director of sales position at a hospitality company. Our client just so happened to be a direct competitor of her employer. When she gave her notice to her boss, he really lost it. He didn't want to lose her. Rather than handling the situation with grace, he took it upon himself to make her final two weeks with him a living hell. He constantly berated her, fished for information about where she was going, and tried to guilt her into staying. But she held strong. Not only did she give him zero information on her plan, she also passed on *three* counteroffers.

Elizabeth had her mind made up, never wavered, and expertly handled a very challenging and uncomfortable situation. Where many people would have cracked, she made her choice and powered through the fallout with tunnel vision. It was admirable. And guess what? Everything worked out in the end. She is thriving in her new position, and so happy that she made the move. She is in a better culture, surrounded by coworkers and supervisors who respect her and have already promoted her.

Had she accepted one of those counteroffers, she would have been stuck in a mediocre situation at best. Even with the significant pay raise her previous boss offered, she'd be showing up to work every day working for someone still fuming over the fact that she almost left. He may never have let it go, and always held it against her.

This candidate stood strong in her conviction, divulged nothing, and refused to fall into the counter-offer trap. As a result, she is better off for it today.

KEY POINTS IN THIS CHAPTER

Salary should be negotiated with tact and only in cases where necessary.

When salary is not up for negotiation, consider other aspects of an offer as bargaining chips.

Whether you are accepting or rejecting an offer, express gratitude and make your decision promptly.

When giving notice, remember: do not answer uncomfortable questions, stay positive, and always offer to stay for two weeks during the transition period.

Beware of counteroffers. Have your mind firmly made up before you formally announce your resignation.

Chapter Seven

—

WORKING WITH AN AGENCY

Everything you need to know about effectively embarking on your own job search is here in this book. You can be successful going it alone armed with the knowledge in these pages, but job hunting *properly* is a lot of work. It requires a serious commitment of your time and energy.

There is another option. You can let professionals do some of the legwork for you. An agency (also called a headhunter, recruiter, or placement firm) is a third party that helps companies (which we call "clients") fill their open positions. Agencies do this by sourcing and vetting candidates, and then referring the ones they feel are a good fit.

An agency can be your best ally in a job search. As you

know, the biggest hurdle candidates face in the hiring process is getting *noticed*; success lies in separating yourself from the fray and getting on the hiring manager's radar. Agencies are hired by their clients who say, "Go find me some great talent." They already have the trust of the hiring company. If a good agency refers you to their client, you will go straight to the top of the list. You want a headhunter pushing for you, because they have the power to get you to the front of the line.

The agency can also be your best friend when it comes to polishing any rough areas and helping you put your best foot forward. They want you to succeed. When you impress their client, they look good, so it's in their best interest to help you make the best impression possible.

AGENCIES WORK FOR CLIENTS, NOT FOR CANDIDATES

If you are thinking about utilizing an agency (or several) in your quest for new employment, there is a critical distinction you must understand and respect. If you have ever worked with a headhunter at some point in your career, you already know this: Agencies work for companies, not candidates. Agencies are job fillers, not job finders. What exactly do I mean by that?

> Agencies work for companies, *not* candidates. Agencies are job fillers, not job finders.

When job seekers reach out to my firm, they often think, "Oh, an agency. They'll market me to a bunch of potential employers and help me find a job." It doesn't work that way. Don't get me wrong, the agencies are on your side; they want to place you. But they can only place a candidate who is a match for a current opening with one of their clients.

An agency's client will call and say, "We're looking for a director of sales with at least five years of experience in the hospitality industry, and excellent leadership skills. They've got to be an A+ personality and have led a small team for at least one year. They also need to live within thirty minutes of the property location and be under the $120,000 salary threshold." Descriptions are usually even more specific than that. Then, it's the agency's job to go out and find candidates who fit this criteria exactly. If that's not you, they can't help you.

Nothing is more irritating to a recruiter or headhunter than when a candidate reaches out to them and says, "I'm looking for a job. Can you help me?" The response will be something like, "I'm happy to take your resume. If a good fit comes along, I'll get back to you." They are not being rude. Actually, they are probably being very sincere. But they make their money by closing successful placements, and to fill those open jobs they need to stay hyper-focused solely on those candidates whom their clients actually want to hire.

Same thing goes once you have an established relationship with an agency. Don't drive your recruiter crazy with LinkedIn messages or emails like, "Hey, just checking in," with all sorts of questions on the progress of their search. There is no search. Yes, the recruiter understands that you're just trying to stay on the radar. While they are sympathetic to that, they are simply too busy to respond to hundreds of messages like this; you're not the only candidate they are working with, and you're not the only one emailing them to "check in."

People ask, "Do you have anything for me?" Meanwhile the recruiter is thinking, "Ugh, I wish this guy would leave me alone! If there were something for him, he would have gotten a call. I already told him, he's in our files and I'll reach out to him if a match pops up."

If you understand this basic concept, it will be appreciated more than you know by the agencies you work with. They will find it downright refreshing if you call them and say, "Hi, I'm on the market for a new position right now and wanted to pass my resume along to you. If you think I could ever be a good fit for something with one of your clients, I hope that you will contact me." Instantly, you will make a good impression, and the recruiter will appreciate working with someone who gets it.

If you reach out to agencies and they do not have anything for you right away, rest assured that you'll wind up in their files. This is a good thing. Recruiters maintain huge data-bases of candidates, and they do reference them when new searches come in. There's no telling when you could be a match for one of their opportunities. It could be days, weeks, months, or even years later. So don't be offended or discouraged if a recruiter tells you that she's put your resume in her database. That's a sign that she is willing to work with you if and when the time is right. She's just waiting on the right fit to come along for you. Until then, sit tight.

Once a potential match comes along, your resume will be flagged and the recruiter will call you to begin the vetting process. *This* is when your relationship with that agency will blossom. Good agencies will do a deep dive into your experience and really get to know you before ever submit-ting your information to one of their clients. They might put you through multiple interviews (by phone, video chat, in person, or a mix of the above), check your ref-erences, ask you to take skills, personality, or behavioral assessments, and more. Whatever their process, respect it. Their goal is to get to know you. If they like you enough to represent you, they will become your biggest advocate when you interview with their client.

DIFFERENT TYPES OF AGENCIES

Some agencies identify as "headhunting" firms, which means that they execute extremely targeted searches. Their purpose and end goal is to surface and present the "needle in a haystack" candidates for very specific opportunities. They tend to focus on executive or director-level positions, or anything that is particularly difficult for any reason. If a company has already taken a crack at filling a role on their own and struck out, that's when they call in a headhunter.

Headhunters generally present a very small number of candidates for any given opportunity, sometimes as few as one or two people. Their vetting process is extremely thorough. They are all about finding and recommending the one person who will be a perfect fit, as opposed to flooding a client with lots of choices and crossing their fingers that they'll like someone. Headhunters are paid handily for their efforts; sometimes as much as 30 percent or more of a placed candidate's base salary. A headhunter is called when a company needs the "big guns" to come in, give their full attention to a search, and deliver an outstanding candidate.

There are also "recruiting" firms, which tend to do a larger volume of placements with a looser process. They might fill all levels of positions, including entry level. Their search methods are broader and their vetting process slightly less intense. They tend to cast wide nets when sourcing candidates. Perhaps they post on job boards, recruit from colleges or job fairs, and ask for referrals.

The goal of a recruiter is still to fill the position at hand, but their clients tend to want to see options. Rather than presenting one or two people to their client for a particular opening, a recruiter might screen thirty people and then pass along the best five or seven resumes for their client to review. If the client is interested in any of those people, they will let the recruiter know, and then proceed with interviews from there.

Recruiting firms typically do a higher volume of lower and mid-level positions, and tend to have larger staffs. For them, the game is more about quantity, and creating a pipeline of candidates for their clients. They are still paid well, but their commission fees are lower than a headhunter's—generally closer to 20 percent.

Some agencies (like mine, for example) are a hybrid. These firms are boutique in size. They provide the level of personal attention and scrutiny one would receive from a headhunter, while also tackling a broad range of searches at reasonable fees. A hybrid firm might work with a smaller client list, but odds are those clients use the agency multiple times per year due to the relationship and trust they have built. Many companies have their go-to recruiters that they turn to every time they have a vacancy.

There are also temp agencies, which are firms that fill temporary positions. Their clients are usually large companies that have varying needs. A temp agency might fill a three-month opening while a permanent employee is out on maternity leave, or a two-week opening while someone is out on vacation.

Some agencies do "temp to perm," meaning that their temporary placements can convert to permanent hires if the client wants to bring them on as a full-time employee. Some fill both temporary and permanent positions. Some agencies are direct hire, while others put candidates on their own payroll. There are many variations.

I am speaking in generalities, but the purpose of this industry synopsis is to give you some idea of the types of companies out there.

TEMP WORK IS NOT FOR LOSERS

When the term "temp work," comes up, people often react with an attitude of, "That's for losers," or "That's for people who can't get a real job." Not the case! Temping is something that I recommend in many cases, particularly for candidates who are fresh out of college and have no idea what they want to do. Temping is also good for anyone who is having trouble landing the right opportunity. Here's why. Positions that originally start out as temp often go permanent. Remember that new mom who took a few months off for maternity leave? Maybe she decides not to come back to work at all. If you're the temp who's been filling her shoes and you've done a good job, guess what? That permanent position might very well be yours.

I've seen plenty of companies who never really planned on hiring through a temp agency wind up so pleased with their interim hire that they offer the job to that person. Why go conduct a full search if they have a perfectly capable person who wants to be there already sitting in the seat?

Even if your temp position does not turn into permanent employment, a great benefit of temping is that you gain exposure to many different companies and work environments. A week here, a month there, two days over there, and so on. Every experience you have will help you figure out what you want in your ideal position and employer. Particularly for younger professionals, this can be a really smart strategy. Having exposure to so many different people, places, and cultures helps anyone get to know themselves better, and develop their list of non-negotiables. And when they put the experience on their resume, they can say they did a two-year stint with the staffing agency, rather than showing fifteen different jobs. But they still get the personal benefits of having worked for fifteen different companies. Temping gives you the opportunity to job hop without being penalized for it!

Unlike headhunters and recruiters, temp agencies will tend to represent pretty much anyone remotely qualified who submits a resume. They have a ton of hours that they need to cover each week, and it's hard to find enough reliable people. Temp agencies are constantly cranking through candidates, and their clients' needs change from day to day. They need people on the bench. Due to a disparity in supply and demand, they wind up having to work with many mediocre (and just plain awful) temps.

If you think that temping for a while might be a good option for you, there's even more good news: you can easily impress by standing out in a sea of average. Walking into a temp agency as a presentable, professional, reliable person who has skills to bring to the table will instantly get you noticed as one of the most impressive people on the roster. You can bet you'll be one of the first people that agency will think of when opportunities come up, and there's a high probability that they will keep you consistently employed.

You should also know that the temp agency's goal will be to get you placed permanently. They make a small hourly fee off the hours that you work as a temp, but they will make a significant commission if they get you hired with their client as a permanent employee. So, your desired end game will be the same.

If you are struggling in your quest for new employment or having a hard time figuring out what you want, be open to temping. Find a reputable agency with good clients and take advantage of what they can offer you: a paycheck, an opportunity to experience working for lots of different companies, and excellent networking. How can you go wrong? Temping just might be the ticket to a rewarding, full-time, permanent position with a fantastic employer— that you never saw coming.

HOW TO SELECT AN AGENCY

If your career is focused on a specific industry, you'll probably have the best luck finding an agency that specializes in the same. They will have the most connections in your field, as well as the most relevant opportunities. Your odds of finding a great match will be strong if you go this route.

Ask around for referrals. Do you know someone who was placed by a headhunter last year? Give that person a call and ask who made the connection. If you are keeping your search under wraps and are worried about confidentiality, you can turn to Google. Search for things like, "head-hunter for the healthcare industry," or "best recruiter in New York." Type in "staffing firm" and your current city, and you'll turn up more results than you'll know what to do with. Then, switch out the city for your industry.

Note that some "best of" lists are pay for play; agencies pay a fee to be on them. So it's likely that your searches may turn up junk as well as some great firms. Just because an agency appears on a "best of" list doesn't mean that they are necessarily well regarded. Use online searches as a starting point, but you'll want to do deeper research on each company you turn up.

There is no need to focus on agencies only in your city. Many placement firms have clients nationwide or at least regionally, so don't limit your search by geography. A headhunter based in California might have the perfect opportunity for you in your home city of Washington, DC. You never know, so be open-minded in terms of geographical location.

CREATE A LIST, DO YOUR RESEARCH, THEN REACH OUT

After you've established a short list of agencies that look interesting to you, go to their websites. Get a sense of what they are all about and research their specialty areas of recruitment. As you come across firms that look like a good fit, you'll want to send them copies of your resume. There may be an email address listed for resumes to be sent, or perhaps an online form of some kind. Whatever their process, follow the instructions.

Basically, you're just getting into the agency's database at this point. It's likely that someone on the inside will briefly lay eyes on your information to see if you're a fit for any of their current openings. If so, they'll call you. If not, they'll stick your resume in their files. Either way, it's a win, because now you're on their radar.

Be aware that there are some disreputable recruiters out there. The recruiting industry in general has a bad rep, and while I hate to say this, it is for good reason. The field is packed with dishonest and careless recruiters who throw resumes around and put very little care into their work. I've heard recruiters as a whole referred to as "used car salesmen." It's disheartening to those of us who do take our careers seriously and are deeply committed to what we do. But it is what it is. Like any business, there are those who are excellent and those who have no business calling themselves professionals. This industry is no different.

When you're choosing agencies to partner with, be selective. Remember that the recruiters you choose will reflect on your own professional reputation. Some recruiters will send hundreds of resumes out on blast, rather than carefully matchmaking the right person to the right job opening. You absolutely want to avoid any agency that operates haphazardly, because you always want to know where your resume is being sent. My firm never submits a resume to any client without a candidate's express approval. Our resumes are stored in a confidential database, and when a match comes our way, we call the suitable candidates and say, "Let's discuss this." That's the respectful and correct way to go about it.

Other firms won't necessarily disclose where your information is going, nor do they make the effort to really get to know you. Make sure you are associating only with firms that represent you in the way that you want and deserve to be represented—professionally and thoughtfully.

Also, you can and should use more than one agency. Why wouldn't you? Your ultimate goal is to find a great opportunity, and the more agencies you have looking out for you, the better your odds. Each firm has different contacts and different clients. You will broaden your reach and your options by working with a handful of agencies as opposed to just one. By the way, you will not offend or annoy a recruiter by working with multiple firms. They will not feel cheated on if they find out you have a relationship with some of their competitors. (If they do, they don't have your best interest at heart—and that's evidence enough that they're not a firm you should be aligning with).

IT'S GO TIME! (AN AGENCY WANTS TO REPRESENT YOU)

When an agency has a match for you, they will call. I cannot tell you how many times I have had candidates say to me, "Wow, we haven't spoken in forever. I can't believe you held onto my information and actually remembered me!" My response is always, "I told you I would." There is a strange magic with recruiters where, even if they haven't talked to you in three years, if a match comes along they will remember you. That's what we get paid to do.

When that call comes, odds are it's going to be a pretty solid fit. So how do you maximize the relationship with your recruiter so that you both win?

PUT IT ALL OUT THERE

When you're talking to an agency (versus an actual

employer), the relationship is different. This person and the firm they work for are your ally in the hiring process. They are your advocate, and they want you to get the job. They are rooting for you because when you win, they win. Treat them like your best friend.

You want to always be brutally honest with your recruiter. Ask questions. Bounce things off them. Tell them about your insecurities. Ask for advice. Get personal. Share your likes and dislikes. Don't want a commute longer than thirty minutes? Tell the recruiter. Prefer working solo rather than on a team? Tell your recruiter. Hate wearing suits and want to work for a company that has a casual dress code? Say so. All those self-reflection gems you came up with back in Chapter 1—share them.

Good recruiters are exceptional matchmakers. The more they know about you, the better match they can make on behalf of you and their client. Because they're not the one actually hiring you, they can help you without bias or judgment.

Agencies have clients who say, "This is a staff accounting job. We want someone to just show up here and do their job and not have ambitions to take over the company one day. They need to stay in their box." And the recruiter will say, "I have the perfect person." So long as everyone is honest, there are no wrong answers. If your preferences and background don't fit one client, they might fit another. You wouldn't want to force it anyway.

Any misrepresentation is likely to place you in a job that is a poor fit. That's bad news all around. Not only will you be miserable, but your recruiter won't look good when you leave in a year because it was a bad match. If you lie to an agency, consider that a bridge permanently burned. Recruiters have zero tolerance for dishonesty and they resent being embarrassed. If you hide your aspirations, take a job, then say, "Oh, surprise! I'm moving to Paris. I know I just took this job two months ago, but I'm leaving in thirty days," you will severely risk the reputation of the recruiter, and they will not forgive you. Never put them in a position like this.

The best thing about the respectable recruiters of the world: They understand discretion better than anyone. If you share openly with them, your secrets are safe. Yes, their onus is technically to their clients, but there are certain lines that they will not cross. They'll never run to an employer and say something unflattering about you. In fact, they'll do exactly the opposite, because you being regarded in a positive light is also a positive reflection on them. So, always be open with your agency. Pretend you're talking to a trusted friend. Be honest and specific about who you are. It will serve both of you well.

THE DIRTY DETAILS

Let's say you spent your last two years hopping between four different jobs. That's not appealing to a prospective employer. Should you hide that from an agency? Nope. Instead, tackle it head-on. Have an open discussion with the recruiter about what happened, and why the job hops occurred. She will help you strategize a better way to present that information. She'll say, "I really appreciate your honesty. Here's how I think we can make this sound more palatable."

Since recruiters know their clients, they also know their limits. They are aware of what the client will tolerate and what they won't. Oftentimes, presenting a candidate in the best light possible is just a matter of repositioning and reframing information. The recruiter is the absolute best person to do that in a way that will be within the boundaries of what her client will deem acceptable.

Recruiters can't help you unless you level with them. Withholding information could lead to a big mess. You could end up interviewing with a client and blowing it if something comes to light that the recruiter didn't have the opportunity to repackage, or coach you through how to handle.

Maybe you have a two-year gap on your resume where you didn't work. Obviously, that's not ideal in the eyes of a potential employer. But if you're open about it, your recruiter can help explain it to the client before your interview. "Listen, this gap is legit. He's not a flake and not unmotivated. He paused his career to care for a sick family member, and he went back to work after she passed away." Then, the employer will be much more likely to consider the candidate. Because they understand the back story and they trust the recruiter, everything changes. If the recruiter didn't exist and the employer just blindly saw a resume with a mysterious two-year gap, they'd probably pass.

Anything major in your personal life that could be an issue should also be shared with your agency. I know it might feel uncomfortable disclosing intimate details to a stranger. But if you've got three kids who have demanding schedules which impact your own work hours, your recruiter needs to know that. If you're going through a divorce and there's a strong chance you could be moving out of state in two months, she'll need to know that, too. You get the idea.

Anything that's potentially life altering or relevant to what you can and cannot commit to needs to be out in the open early. Remember, agencies have lots of opportunities available all the time, sometimes even flex work. But if they are matchmaking without knowing your full story, they will be misguided (or just plain shooting in the dark) with their matchmaking efforts. That won't turn out well for either of you.

DEAL-BREAKERS

As much as an agency is in your corner, there are some deal-breakers that will cause them not to submit you to a client or represent you at all. For example, if you've been fired from a previous employer or you have legitimately bad references, a good recruiter will not risk their reputation by sticking their neck out for you. References are generally checked as a matter of protocol, so if they turn up anything negative, that's going to be an issue.

Another deal-breaker is if a candidate is just plain unlikeable. If someone is an irritant, not self-aware, unprofessional, sloppy, or otherwise incapable of making a good impression on a client, again, a good recruiter will not risk their own reputation, no matter how solid a candidate's qualifications are.

PROMPT COMMUNICATION

When an agency calls on you for a specific opportunity, they want to know that you are motivated to pursue it. If you take two days to respond to their message, it better be for good reason. Yes, life happens, but the delay also sends the signal that you're not that interested. Worse, the recruiter will wonder if it's an indicator of future behavior.

When a recruiter calls, pick up the phone immediately or return the call as soon as possible. Show them, through your *actions*, that you are sincere in your interest and committed to the process. They don't want to waste their own energy on someone who doesn't know what they want, or who is generally unmotivated.

A lack of promptness in communication makes recruiters nervous. They will think, "What if my client asks me to set up an interview with this person on short notice, and I can't reach them?" The recruiter needs to know that the two of you are in this together, and that you will be easily accessible to them throughout the submission and interview process. You are a team and communication is key.

TAKE YOUR AGENCY'S ADVICE—ALWAYS

Whatever advice you receive from your agency, take it to the bank. Their goal is the same as yours: getting you placed in an opportunity where you will be really happy and well suited. To get across the finish line, a recruiter might advise his candidate on every aspect of getting hired, from resume tweaks to wardrobe suggestions to what to say or not say in the interview.

The feedback and advice they are giving you is for a reason and from a well-informed vantage point. They have access to the secret preferences of the employer, which is invaluable. Whey they advise you to do something, say something, wear something, whatever the case may be, take it seriously! This is inside baseball and just might be the key to landing the position you want. The recruiter knows what you do not. Their pearls of wisdom can make all the difference.

When they give you advice, it's not a suggestion. They are telling you, politely, what you need to do, focus on, and be aware of to make a good impression on the employer. If you want the job, heed the advice—to the letter.

PLAYING THE LONG GAME

Always approach your interactions with agencies in the mindset of building a long-term relationship. Sure, it's great if they can place you quickly, but you want to stay in their good graces for the long haul. You never know when that perfect job opportunity will come their way.

Some candidates worry that if a recruiter puts them up for a job and then they don't get it, it will tarnish the recruiter's opinion of them. This couldn't be further from the truth. There is no shame in being passed over for an opportunity (or two or three). We know that employers reject wonderful, talented candidates all the time for reasons beyond anyone's control. Personally, if I like someone (and assuming they did not violate a deal-breaker or make a terrible impression with my client), I will always be willing to work with them again, even if they were rejected more than once.

When an employer says no, it's disappointing for the candidate and the recruiter. But recruiters are a resilient breed. We bounce back quickly. We'll say, "Okay, that wasn't the right fit, but I like this guy and would totally work with him again. Something else will come along." It is not at all unusual for an agency to represent the same person multiple times until the right client hires them.

We tend to have this attitude because most of the time candidates aren't rejected because of some egregious issue. Typically, it's just a matter of our client preferring someone else. If the "better" candidate hadn't been in the mix, the other one might have received the offer. So rejection is not a demerit in the recruiter's eyes.

RECRUITERS APPRECIATE GRATITUDE, TOO

When an agency successfully places you with your new employer and life moves forward, it's easy to forget about the person or the team who helped get you that job. Like anyone else, recruiters like feeling appreciated. From time to time over the years, my candidates have sent me handwritten notes, and those are always very meaningful. To this day, I have kept every note I have received.

If you are lucky enough to find a stellar recruiter who has your back and gets you placed, remember to stop and thank her. Without her making the initial connection and staying in your corner, you wouldn't have landed where you are. Showing appreciation will make her feel good; it's just the right thing to do. Besides, you just might need her assistance again someday in the future. Let her know how grateful you are, and I promise you, it will endear you to her forever.

KEY POINTS IN THIS CHAPTER

Agencies are job fillers, not job finders; they work for companies, not for candidates.

Be open to all types of agencies, including those who do temp to perm if you are struggling in your search.

Do your research on agencies before blindly submitting your resume. Focus on those that are reputable and likely to have clients who could be good potential employers for you.

Your agency will be your best ally in the hiring process. Be open, honest, respectful, appreciative, and reliable in your dealings with them. Treat your recruiter like a close friend.

CONCLUSION

My fifteen years (and counting) in the hiring arena have been a fascinating ride. I have seen and heard it all. I have also developed great empathy for both sides of the hiring equation, employers and candidates alike.

Hiring is a stressful process for all involved. Candidates want to feel acknowledged, valued, and rewarded for their talents. They are tired of coming up short, without answers as to why they weren't hired. Meanwhile, employers are just trying to do what's right for their companies, to the extent that they know how. They may not always run their processes perfectly or communicate as well as they should or even make the right choice in the end. But they are human, too, and their decisions are complex—with high stakes. They are trying their best, trust me.

I believe that if both sides had a healthier dose of patience and compassion for the other, we would see far more effective hiring processes. That means happier people and better-quality results.

Complicated as it all may be, here's the great news: As a candidate, you have so much more control over how employers perceive you (and whether or not you get hired) than you might think. Most rejections happen for reasons that are completely preventable. People don't fail to get selected because of who they are, they fail because of what they don't know. Winning at the hiring game is actually simple, once you understand how to play it.

> Winning at the hiring game is actually simple, once you understand how to play it.

If you have your heart set on a specific job opportunity, stick with the process. Be positive, convey relevance and enthusiasm consistently, and project a polished and professional image. Always put your best foot forward, no matter what. Once you are selected and begin your new position (the *right* position), you'll feel so happy and focused that you won't even care anymore how long and winding the path might have been to get there.

MAKE ME PROUD

Today you walk away with insider knowledge of how and

why employers make actual, real-world hiring selections. This is powerful insight that can change your career and your life; but simply understanding how it all works is not enough.

To secure the job you have your eye on, you must actively apply the tips, tricks, and principles provided herein. I promise you, if you do so diligently and consistently, you will see a dramatic and immediate uptick in your success rate.

Put in the effort. It will pay off in spades.

Once you have a taste of being "in demand," there is no greater feeling. The responses to your applications, the interview requests, the callbacks, the messages from recruiters, and the job offers—all of it will feel downright phenomenal. Revel in it! And don't forget to take a moment to acknowledge yourself for the tremendous progress you've made.

So, the time has come to go forth, and attack that job search of yours with a newfound sense of empowerment. You now have the knowledge and tools to snag the opportunities you want and deserve. You're in the driver's seat. I sincerely hope that this book helps take you exactly where you want to go.

ACKNOWLEDGMENTS

To My Clients and Candidates - Simply put, this book would not exist if it weren't for you. It has been an honor watching your stories play out over the years and helping you navigate your journeys. Those collective experiences are the very fabric of which this manuscript is made. Thank you for everything that you have taught me.

To My Parents - It has been said that before we begin each lifetime, we choose our parents. Whether that's true or not, I hit the lottery with the two of you. Thank you for always supporting me without hesitation in all my endeavors and for the tremendous opportunities that you have given me. I love you.

To My "Girls" at Ducci & Associates - Alexis, Kristi, and Abagale, I am so damn lucky to have the most incredible colleagues on the planet. You are brilliant and beautiful, and your support and friendship mean the world to me. Thank you for keeping the business humming along during the many months I was otherwise consumed by the writing of this book. There is no one else with whom I would rather be on this professional journey. Team Ducci all the way. XO

To the Special Teachers – Thank you to those few special professors over the years who took a sincere interest in me, both as a person and as a writer. While it would have been easy for you to overlook "the quiet kid," instead you saw the value, talent, and potential in me—and convinced me of the same. From the bottom of my heart, thank you for believing in me when others did not. I cannot imagine a greater gift.

To Gary – When this manuscript met the approval of the most unabashedly opinionated person I know (you), that's when I knew it had to be good! Thank you for your continued support, counsel, true friendship, and unwavering loyalty year after year. Having you firmly in my corner inspires me every day and means more to me than you will ever know. Thank you for being there.

To Clarisa – You continuously encourage me to do bigger and be better. I am so grateful to have a cheerleader like you! You will forever be the spark that got *Almost Hired* rolling. Thank you.

To My Publishing Team – Katherine, Chris, Erin, and Barbara, I couldn't have asked for a more talented (and fun!) group of professionals to guide me through the process of writing my first book. You made what was initially a very daunting project truly enjoyable, with an end result that has exceeded my expectations. Thank you for your expert guidance.

To My Four-Legged Best Friends – Pumbaa, Sadie, and Steve (you knew I could never leave you out!), each of you bring so much joy and Zen into my life. Thank you for your companionship and your unconditional love.

ABOUT THE AUTHOR

 **JACKIE DUCCI** is the founder and CEO of Ducci & Associates, an East Coast-based talent acquisition agency servicing Fortune 500 clients nationwide. A natural and talented hiring expert with a guiding belief that great companies begin with great employees, Jackie consistently earns the respect and trust of clients and candidates alike with her piercing insight and can-do attitude. Her firm boasts an astounding 90 percent success rate placing candidates in long-term positions.

Outside of work, Jackie's passion has always been animals. She is an avid equestrian who actively trains and competes her own horse in dressage at the regional level, a "dog mom" to her two beloved bulldogs (Pumbaa and Sadie), and a dedicated supporter of various animal-related charities. Jackie obtained a bachelor of arts degree from The Catholic University of America.

Made in the USA
Monee, IL
11 July 2021